DYNAMITE ENTERTAINMENT
AND PANDEMIC STUDIOS PRESENT

MERCENARIES

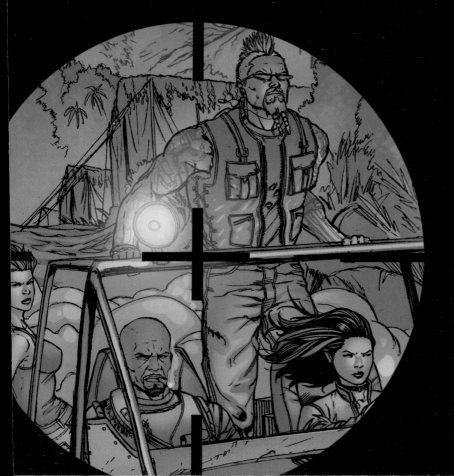

® ENTERTAINMENT

WWW.DYNAMITEENTERTAINMENT.COM

NICK BARRUCCI • PRESIDENT
JUAN COLLADO • CHIEF OPERATING OFFICER
JOSEPH RYBANDT • DIRECTOR OF MARKETING
JOSH JOHNSON • CREATIVE DIRECTOR
JASON ULLMEYER • GRAPHIC DESIGNER

FOR MORE INFORMATION ON PANDEMIC'S MERCENARIES 2
WORLD IN FLAMES, VISIT **WWW.MERCS2.COM**

FOR MORE INFORMATION AND DOWNLOADS, VISIT
WWW.DYNAMITEENTERTAINMENT.COM

First Printing
SOFTCOVER ISBN-10: 9-133305-71-1   ISBN-13: 9-781933-305714
10 9 8 7 6 5 4 3 2 1

DYNAMITE ENTERTAINMENT
AND PANDEMIC STUDIOS PRESENT

MERCENARIES ™

Chris Jacobs. Jennifer Mui. Mattias Nilsson. Each a skilled and deadly warrior, but when you put them together, you have the best of the best... for a price! They are the Mercenaries and, along with operative Fiona Taylor, their latest mission puts them up against the Chinese military in a desperate gamble to rescue one of their own...

Written By:
BRIAN REED

Art By:
EDGAR SALAZAR

Colored By:
ROMULO FAJARDO JR.

Lettered By:
SIMON BOWLAND

Collection And Issue Covers By:
MICHAEL TURNER with
PETER STEIGERWALD

Special Thanks To:
CAMERON BROWN, JONATHAN ZAMKOFF, COURTNEY CHU, RICK VISCARIELLO, JESSE TAYLOR, WILLIE ROSAS, MARK SPENNER, JOSH RESNICK, GREG BORRUD, GREG RICHARDSON, BRAD FOXHOVEN, ANDREW GOLDMAN, PAUL LAUHER, CJ PROBER, DAVID ROSEN

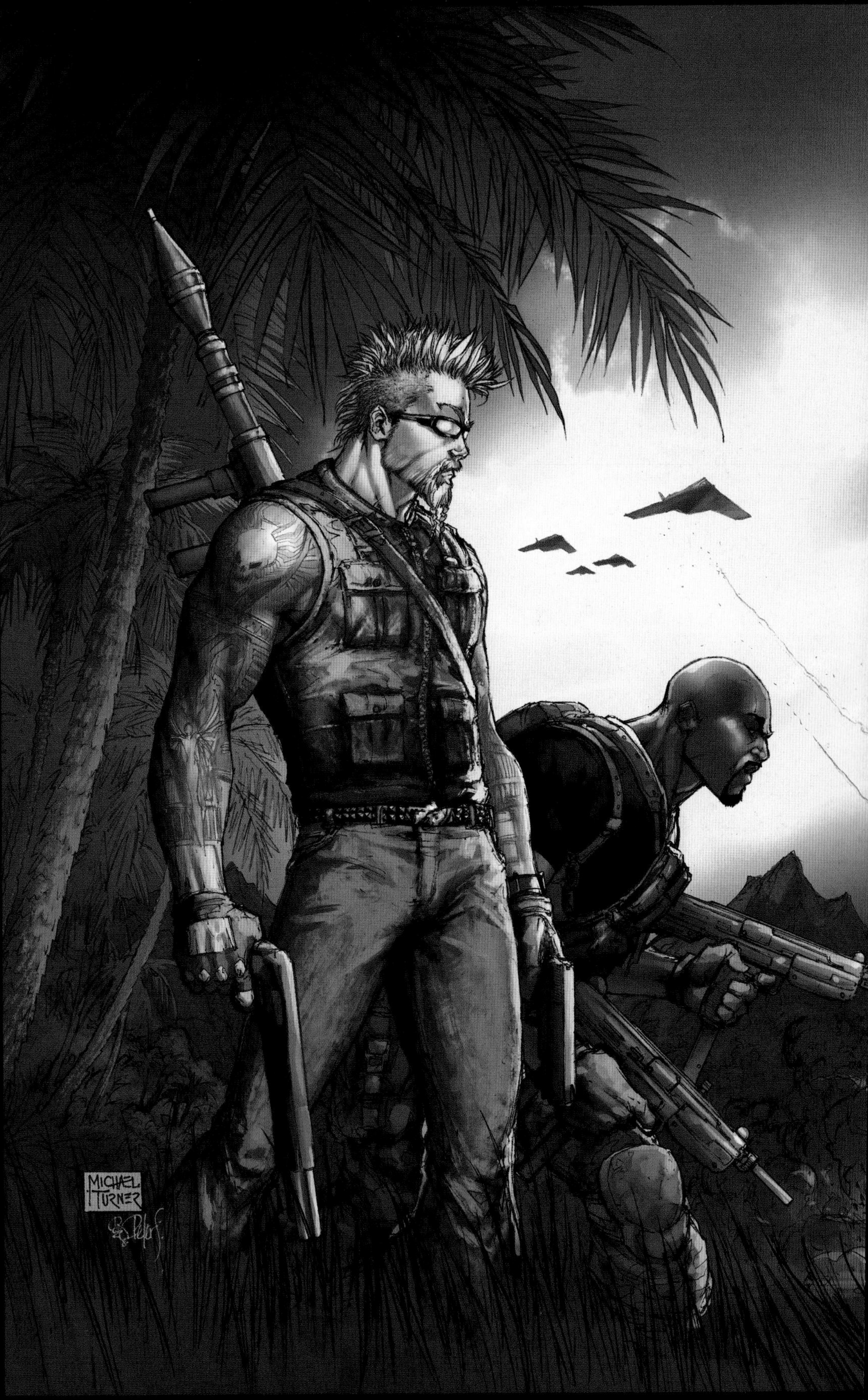
MICHAEL TURNER

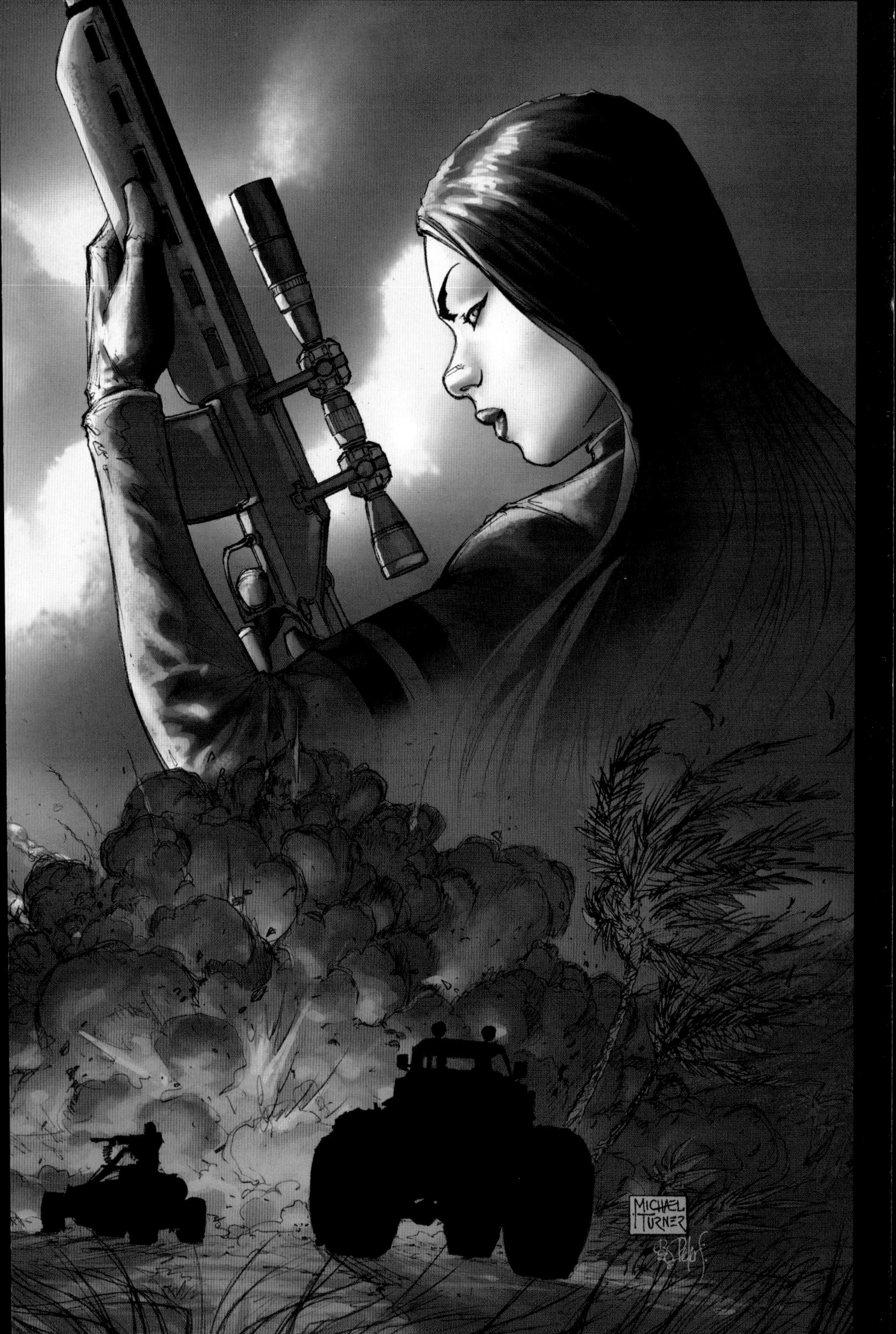
MICHAEL TURNER

CHAPTER ONE

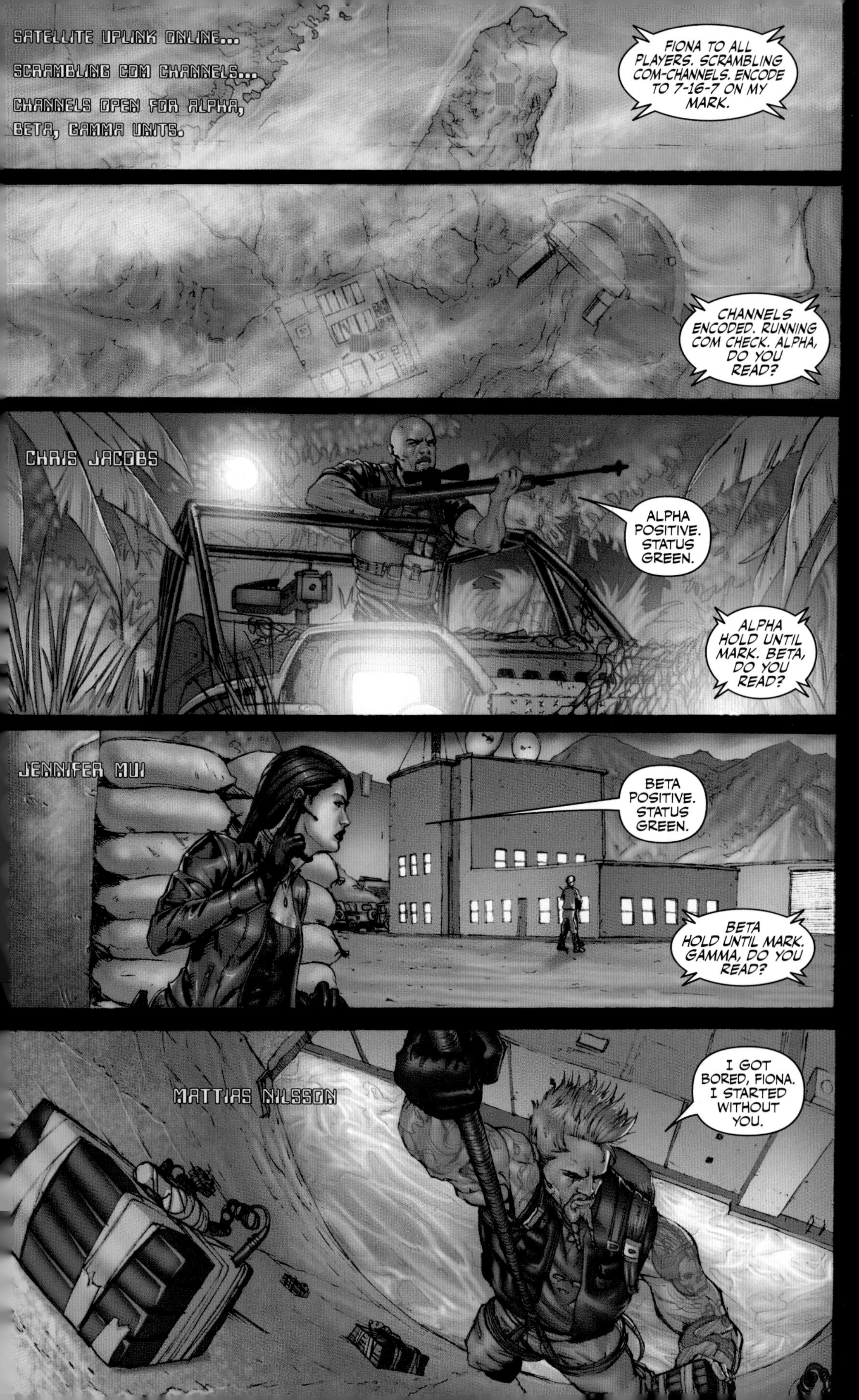
SATELLITE UPLINK ONLINE...
SCRAMBLING COM CHANNELS...
CHANNELS OPEN FOR ALPHA, BETA, GAMMA UNITS.
FIONA TO ALL PLAYERS. SCRAMBLING COM-CHANNELS. ENCODE TO 7-16-7 ON MY MARK.
CHANNELS ENCODED. RUNNING COM CHECK. ALPHA, DO YOU READ?
CHRIS JACOBS
ALPHA POSITIVE. STATUS GREEN.
ALPHA HOLD UNTIL MARK. BETA, DO YOU READ?
JENNIFER MUI
BETA POSITIVE. STATUS GREEN.
BETA HOLD UNTIL MARK. GAMMA, DO YOU READ?
MATTIAS NILSSON
I GOT BORED, FIONA. I STARTED WITHOUT YOU.

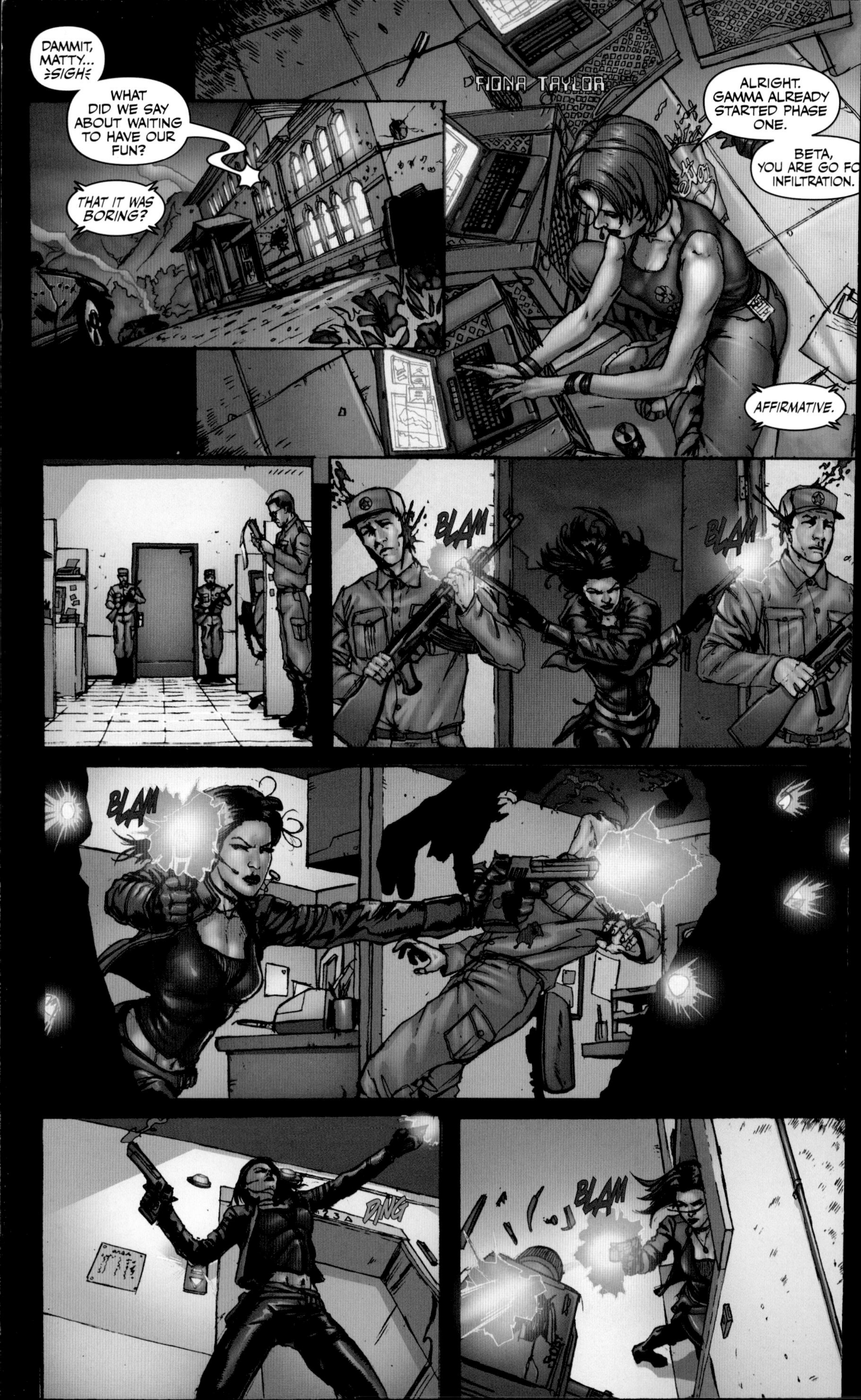
DAMMIT, MATTY... ≶SIGH≷
WHAT DID WE SAY ABOUT WAITING TO HAVE OUR FUN?
THAT IT WAS BORING?
FIONA TAYLOR
ALRIGHT. GAMMA ALREADY STARTED PHASE ONE.
BETA, YOU ARE GO FO INFILTRATION.
AFFIRMATIVE.
BLAM
BLAM
BLAM
DING
BLAM

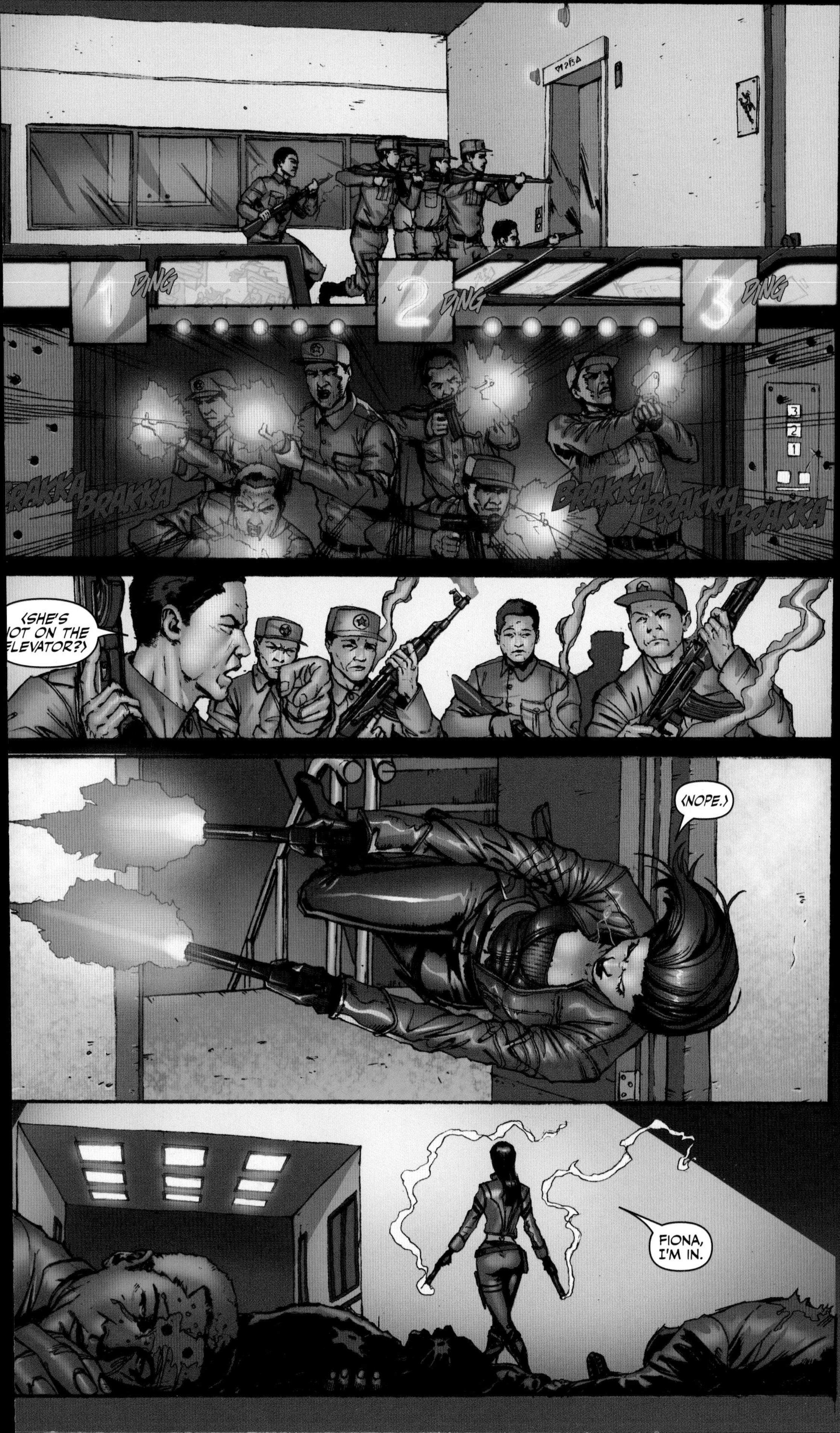

1
DING
2
DING
3
DING
BRAKKA
BRAKKA
BRAKKA
BRAKKA
BRAKKA
3
2
1
‹SHE'S NOT ON THE ELEVATOR?›
‹NOPE.›
FIONA, I'M IN.

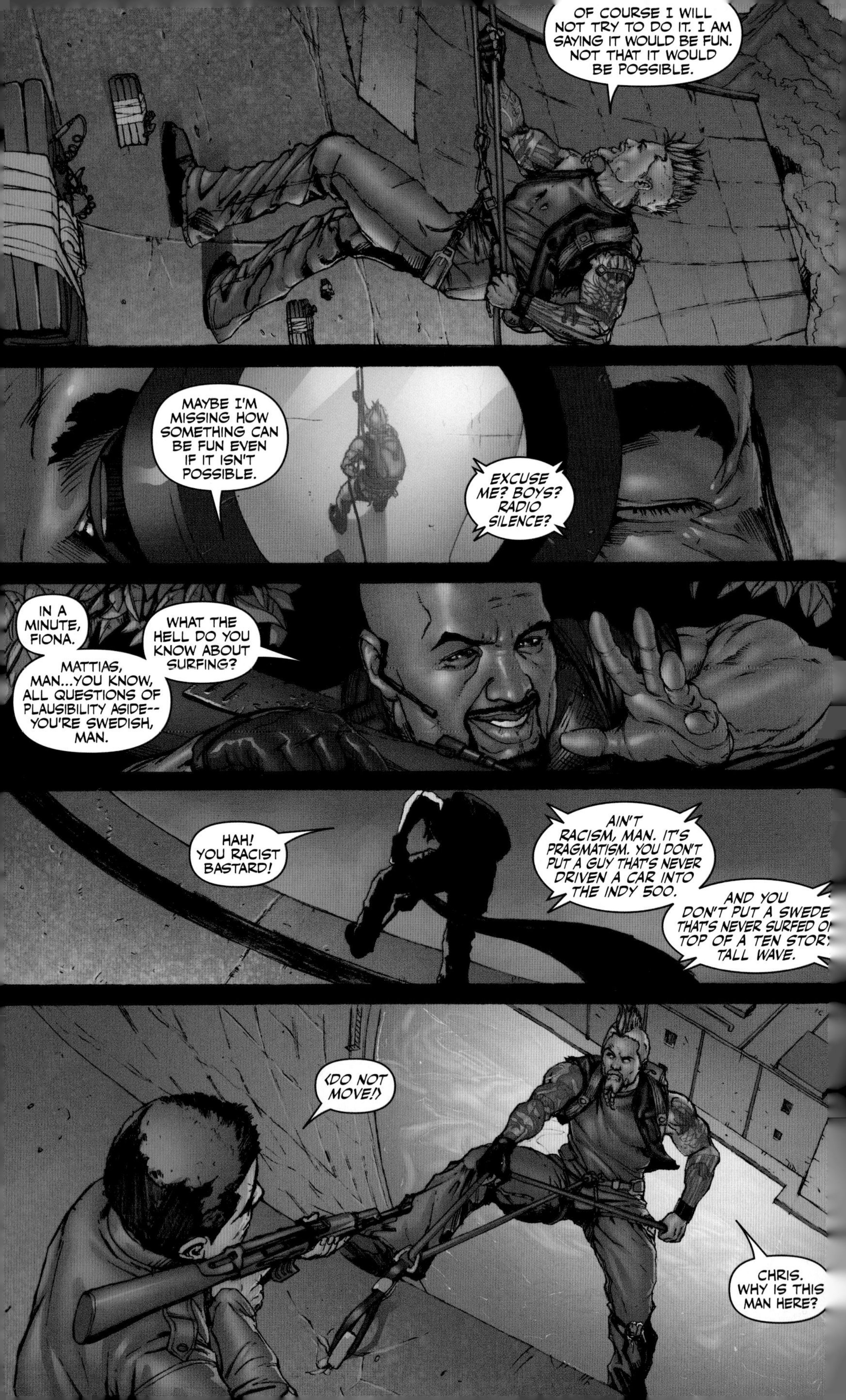
OF COURSE I WILL NOT TRY TO DO IT. I AM SAYING IT WOULD BE FUN. NOT THAT IT WOULD BE POSSIBLE.
MAYBE I'M MISSING HOW SOMETHING CAN BE FUN EVEN IF IT ISN'T POSSIBLE.
EXCUSE ME? BOYS? RADIO SILENCE?
IN A MINUTE, FIONA.
WHAT THE HELL DO YOU KNOW ABOUT SURFING?
MATTIAS, MAN...YOU KNOW, ALL QUESTIONS OF PLAUSIBILITY ASIDE-- YOU'RE SWEDISH, MAN.
HAH! YOU RACIST BASTARD!
AIN'T RACISM, MAN. IT'S PRAGMATISM. YOU DON'T PUT A GUY THAT'S NEVER DRIVEN A CAR INTO THE INDY 500.
AND YOU DON'T PUT A SWEDE THAT'S NEVER SURFED OF TOP OF A TEN STORY TALL WAVE.
<DO NOT MOVE!>
CHRIS. WHY IS THIS MAN HERE?

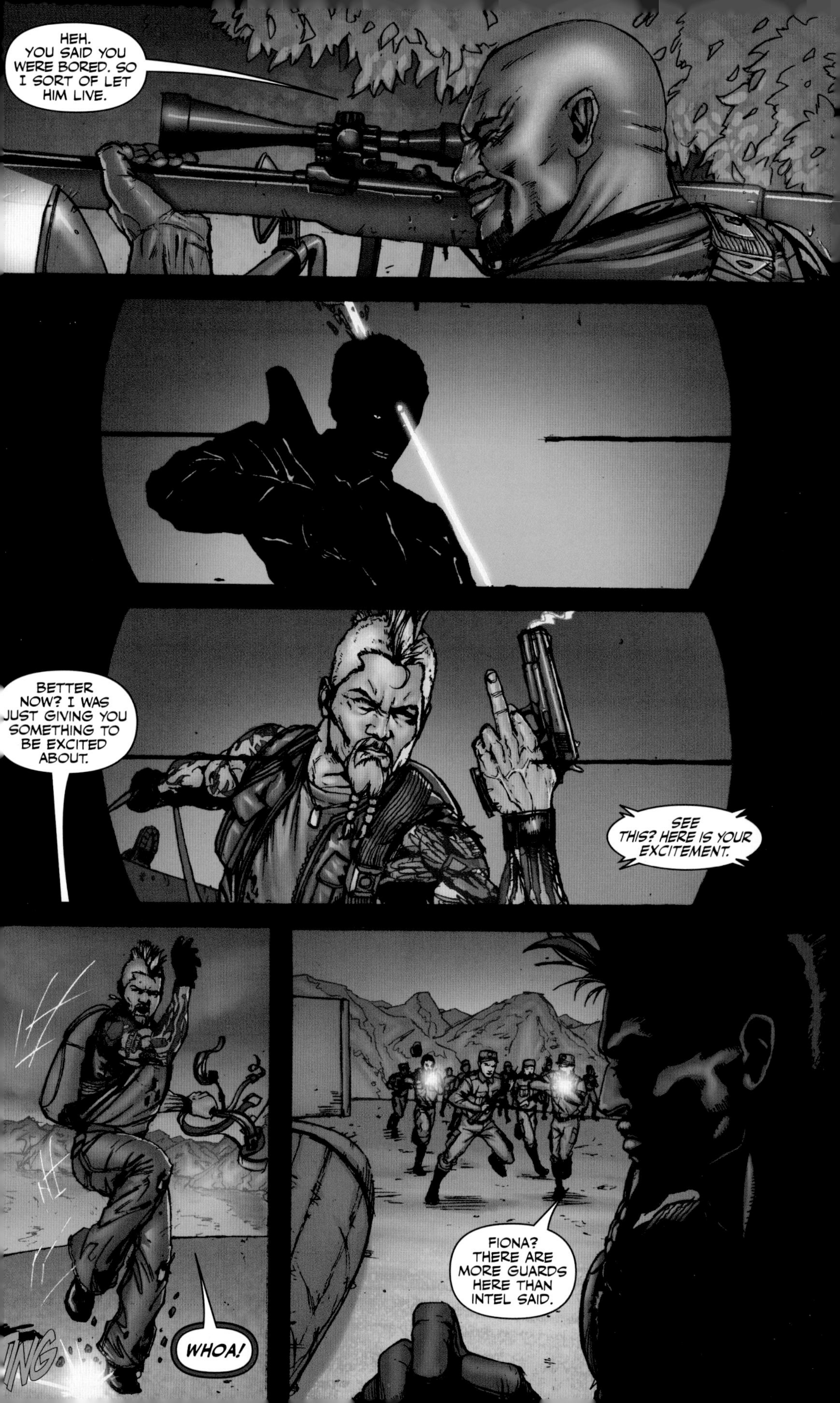
HEH. YOU SAID YOU WERE BORED. SO I SORT OF LET HIM LIVE.
BETTER NOW? I WAS JUST GIVING YOU SOMETHING TO BE EXCITED ABOUT.
SEE THIS? HERE IS YOUR EXCITEMENT.
WHOA!
FIONA? THERE ARE MORE GUARDS HERE THAN INTEL SAID.

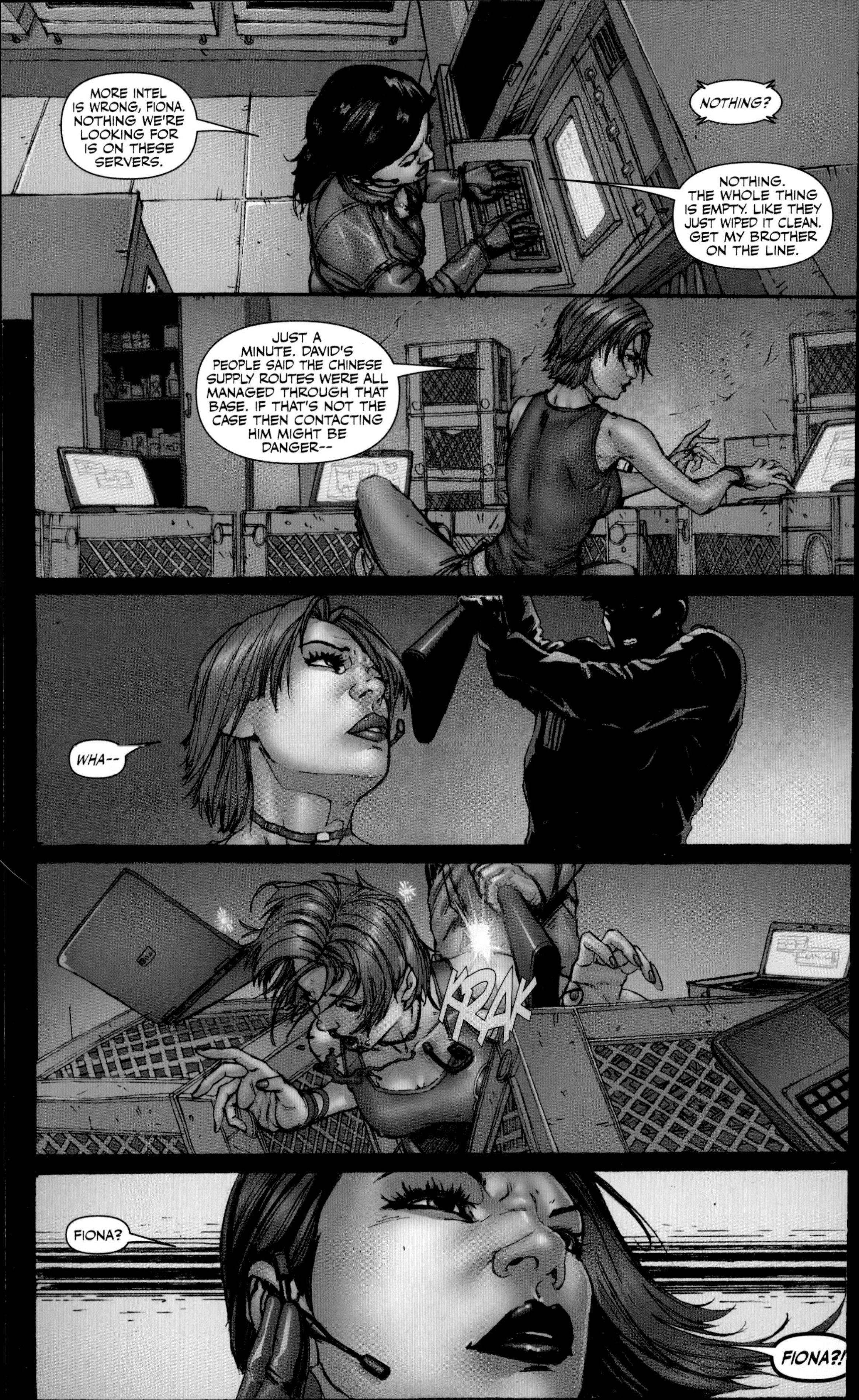
MORE INTEL IS WRONG, FIONA. NOTHING WE'RE LOOKING FOR IS ON THESE SERVERS.
NOTHING?
NOTHING. THE WHOLE THING IS EMPTY. LIKE THEY JUST WIPED IT CLEAN. GET MY BROTHER ON THE LINE.
JUST A MINUTE. DAVID'S PEOPLE SAID THE CHINESE SUPPLY ROUTES WERE ALL MANAGED THROUGH THAT BASE. IF THAT'S NOT THE CASE THEN CONTACTING HIM MIGHT BE DANGER--
WHA--
KRAK
FIONA?
FIONA?!

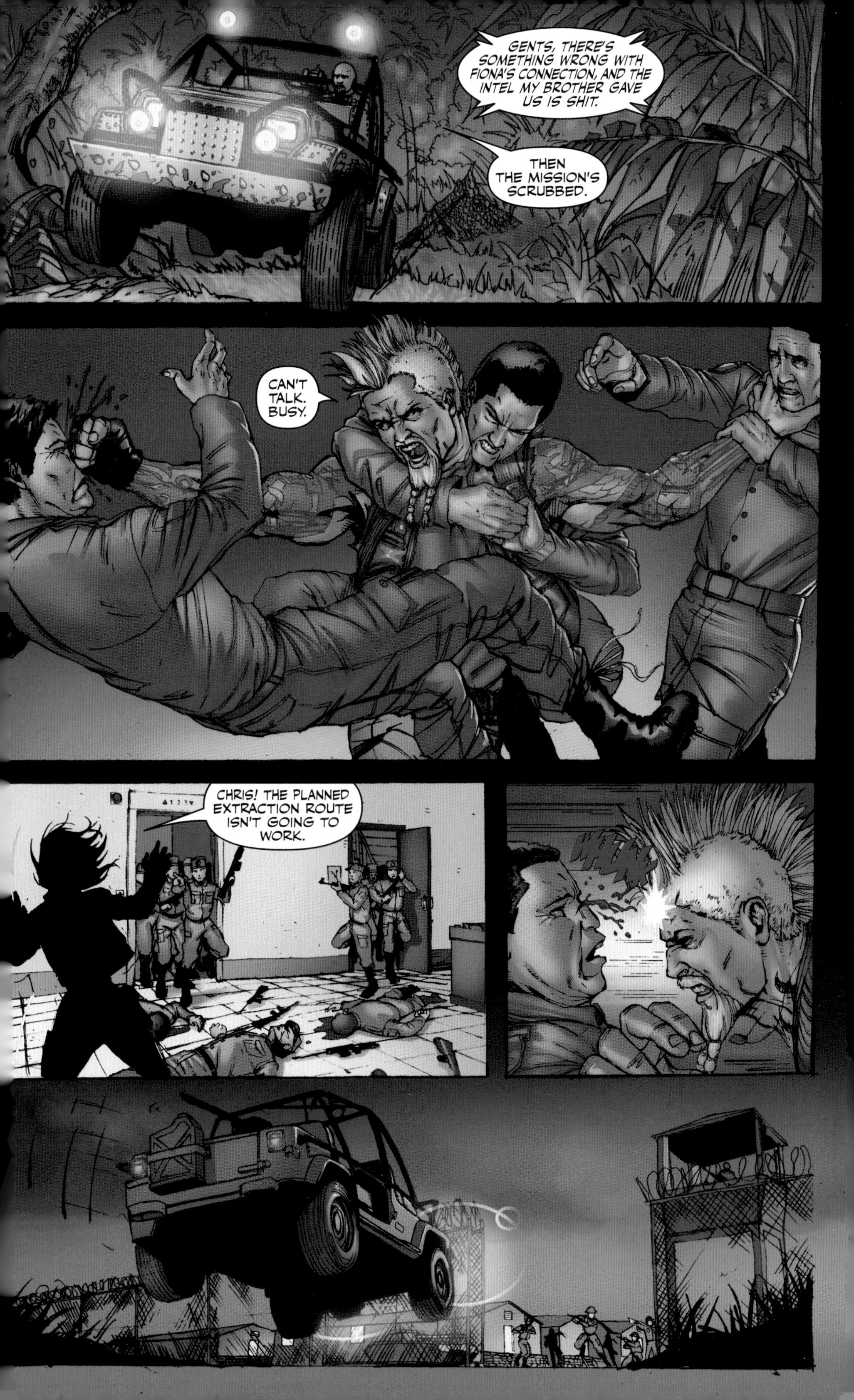
GENTS, THERE'S SOMETHING WRONG WITH FIONA'S CONNECTION, AND THE INTEL MY BROTHER GAVE US IS SHIT.
THEN THE MISSION'S SCRUBBED.
CAN'T TALK. BUSY.
CHRIS! THE PLANNED EXTRACTION ROUTE ISN'T GOING TO WORK.

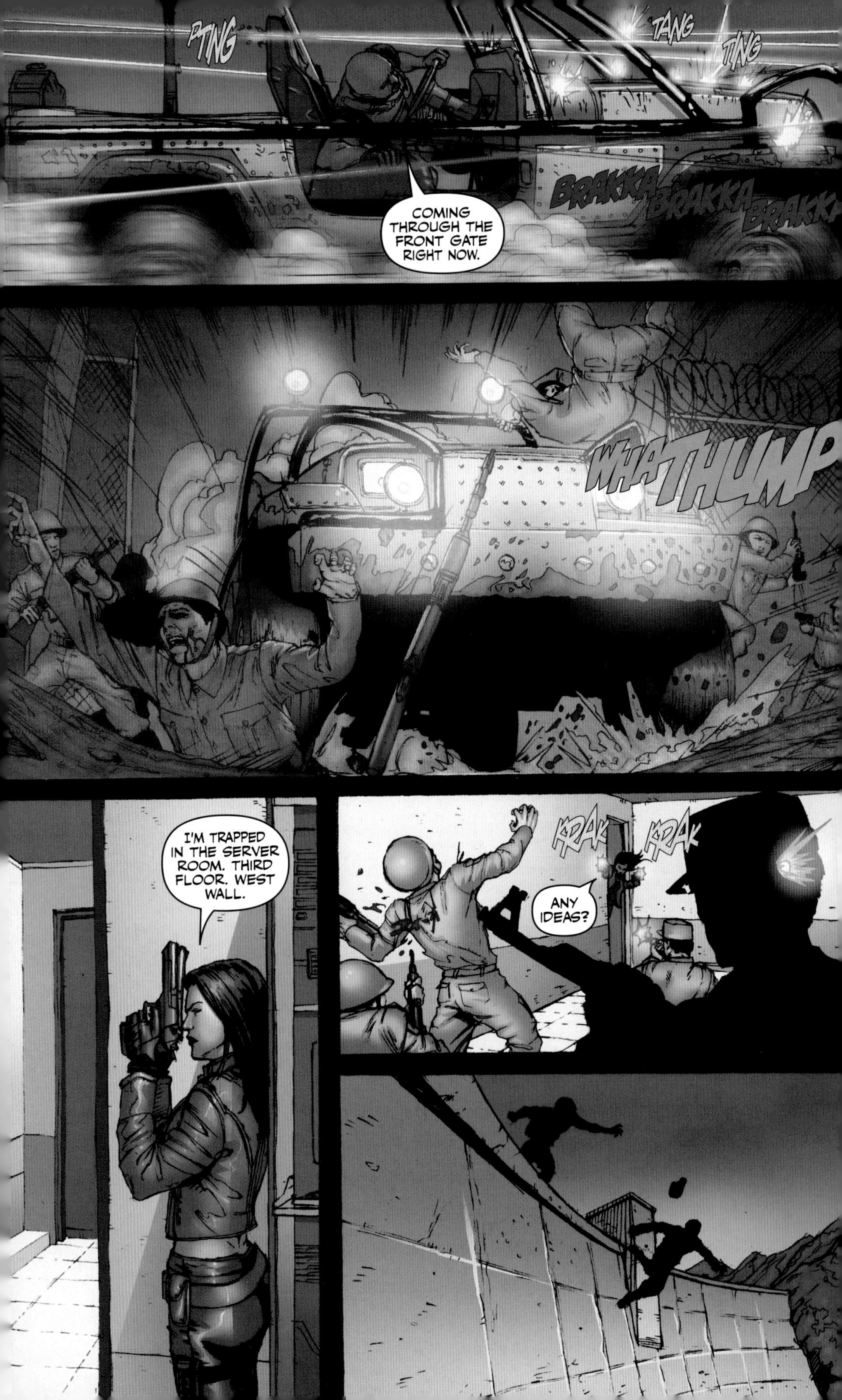
PTING
TANG
TING
BRAKKA BRAKKA BRAKKA
COMING THROUGH THE FRONT GATE RIGHT NOW.
WHATHUMP
I'M TRAPPED IN THE SERVER ROOM. THIRD FLOOR. WEST WALL.
KRAK
KRAK
ANY IDEAS?

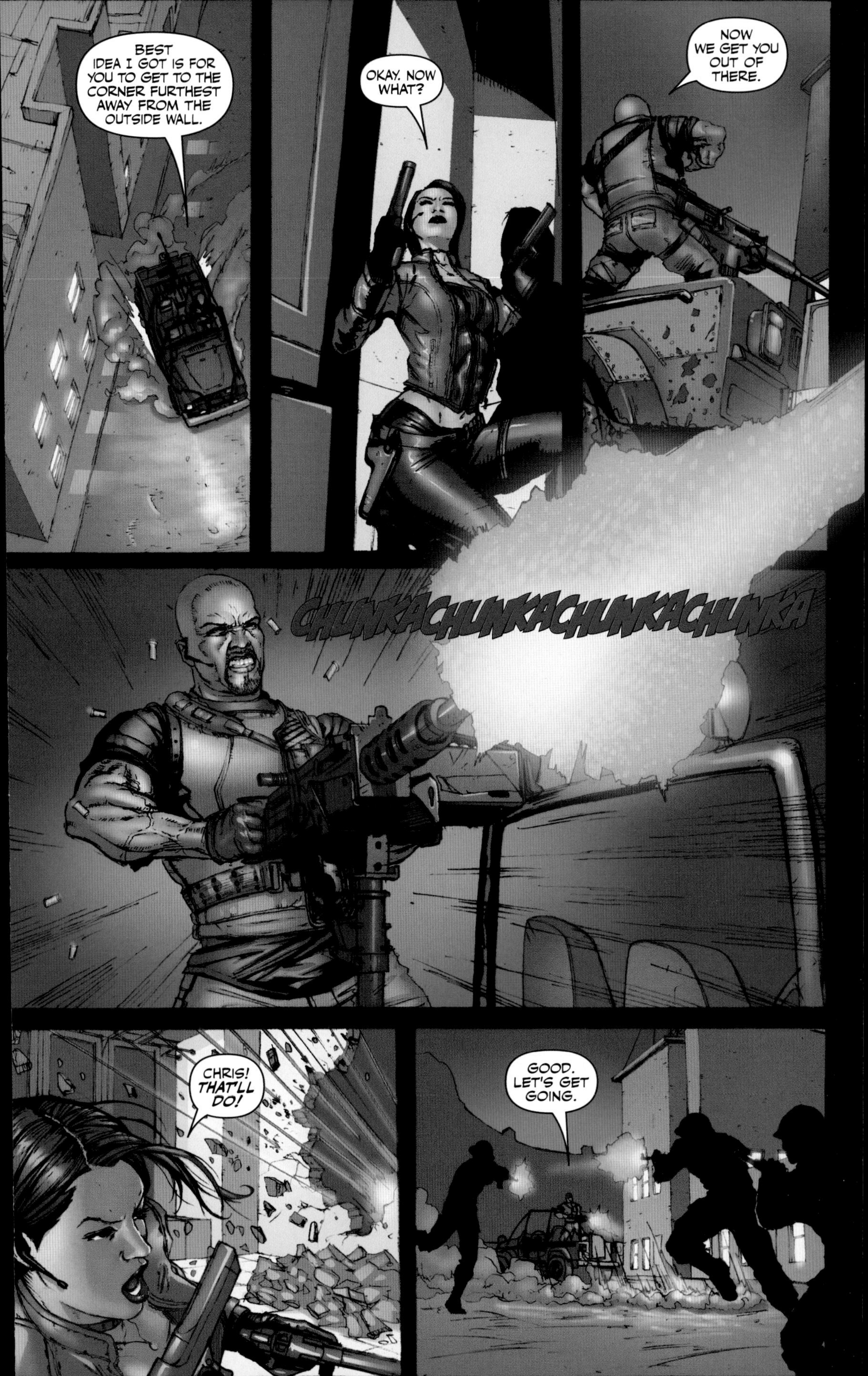
BEST IDEA I GOT IS FOR YOU TO GET TO THE CORNER FURTHEST AWAY FROM THE OUTSIDE WALL.
OKAY. NOW WHAT?
NOW WE GET YOU OUT OF THERE.
CHUNKACHUNKACHUNKACHUNKA
CHRIS! *THAT'LL DO!*
GOOD. LET'S GET GOING.

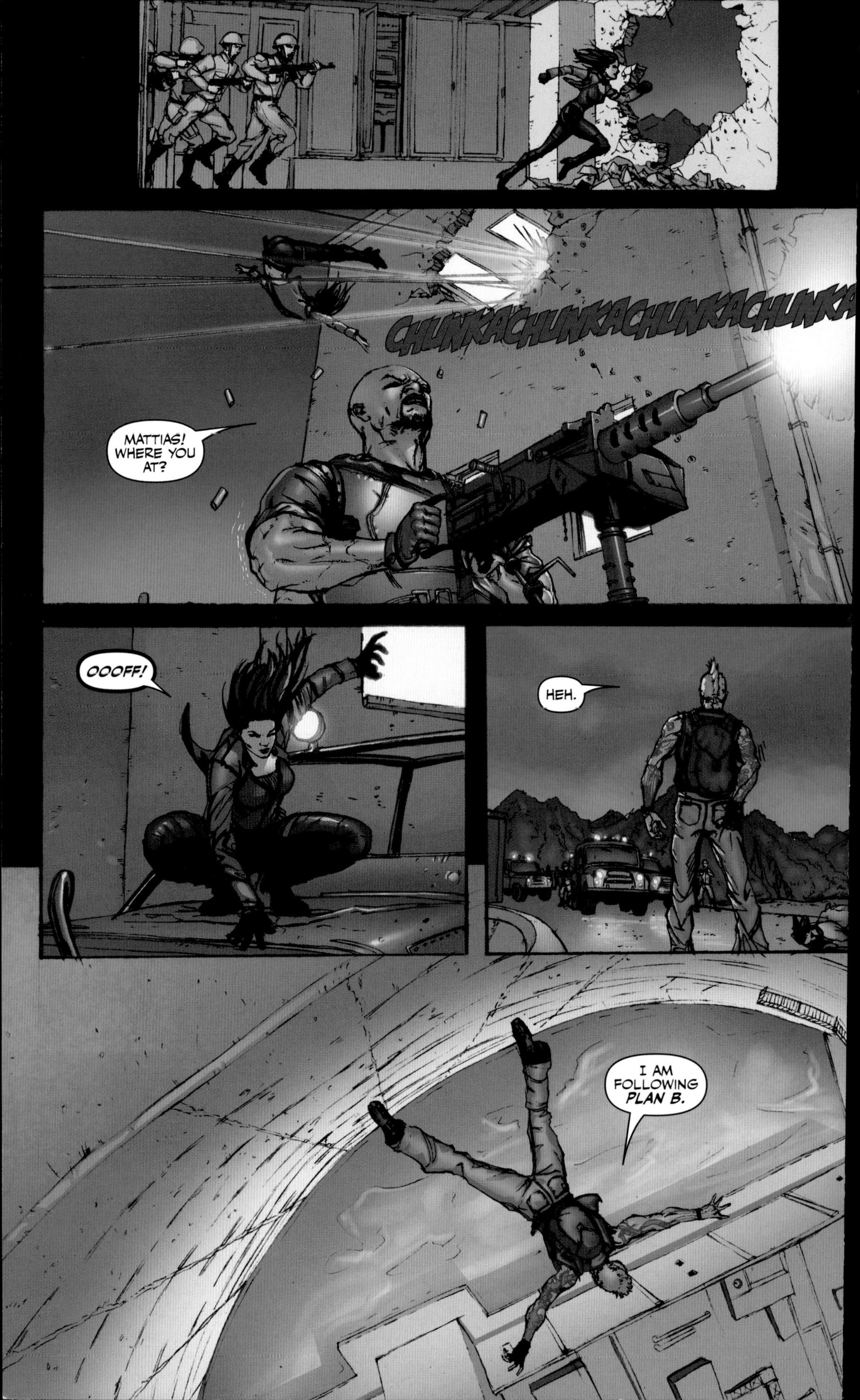
CHUNKACHUNKACHUNKACHUNKA
MATTIAS! WHERE YOU AT?
OOOFF!
HEH.
I AM FOLLOWING PLAN B.

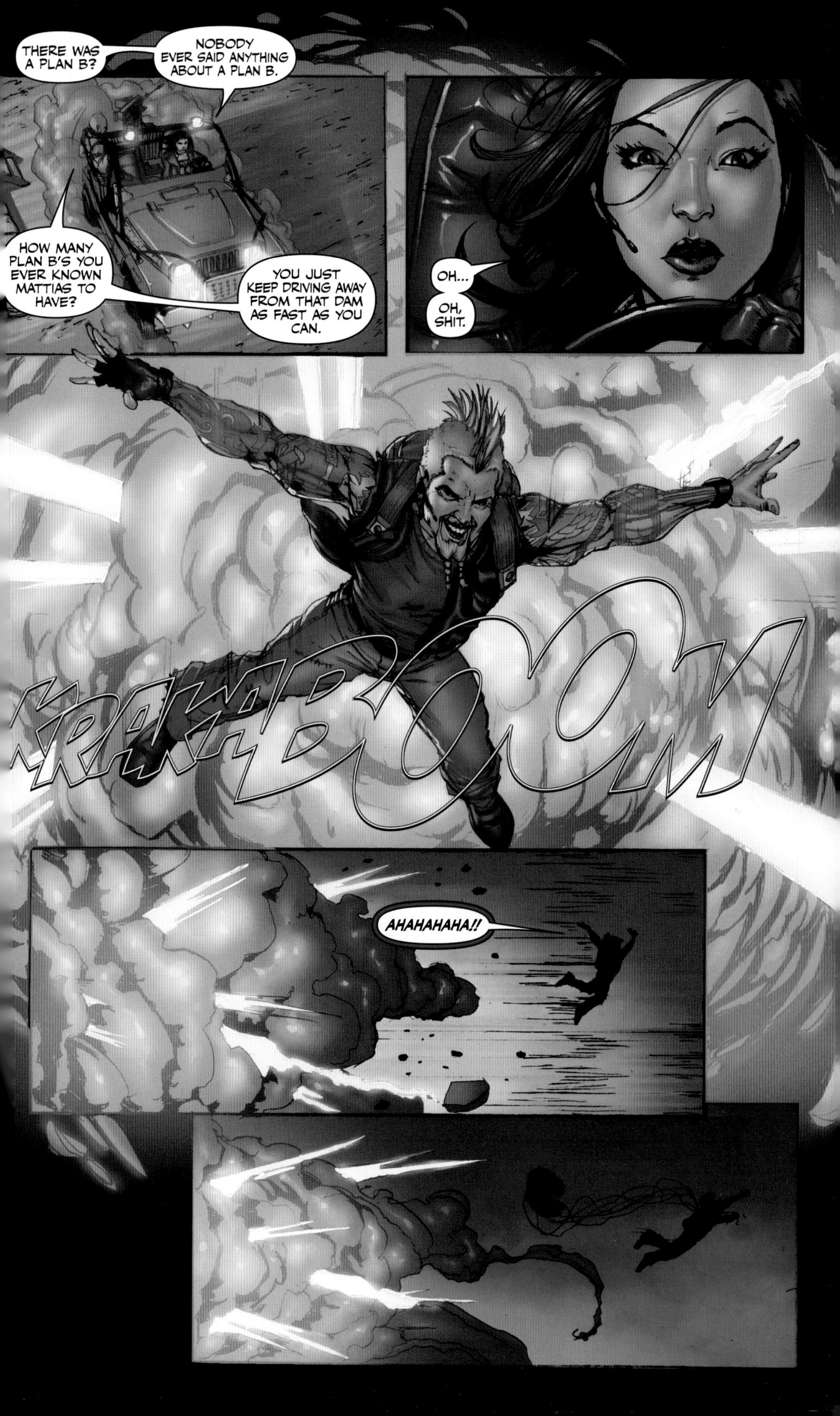
THERE WAS A PLAN B?
NOBODY EVER SAID ANYTHING ABOUT A PLAN B.
HOW MANY PLAN B'S YOU EVER KNOWN MATTIAS TO HAVE?
YOU JUST KEEP DRIVING AWAY FROM THAT DAM AS FAST AS YOU CAN.
OH...
OH, SHIT.
KRAKABOOM
AHAHAHAHA!!

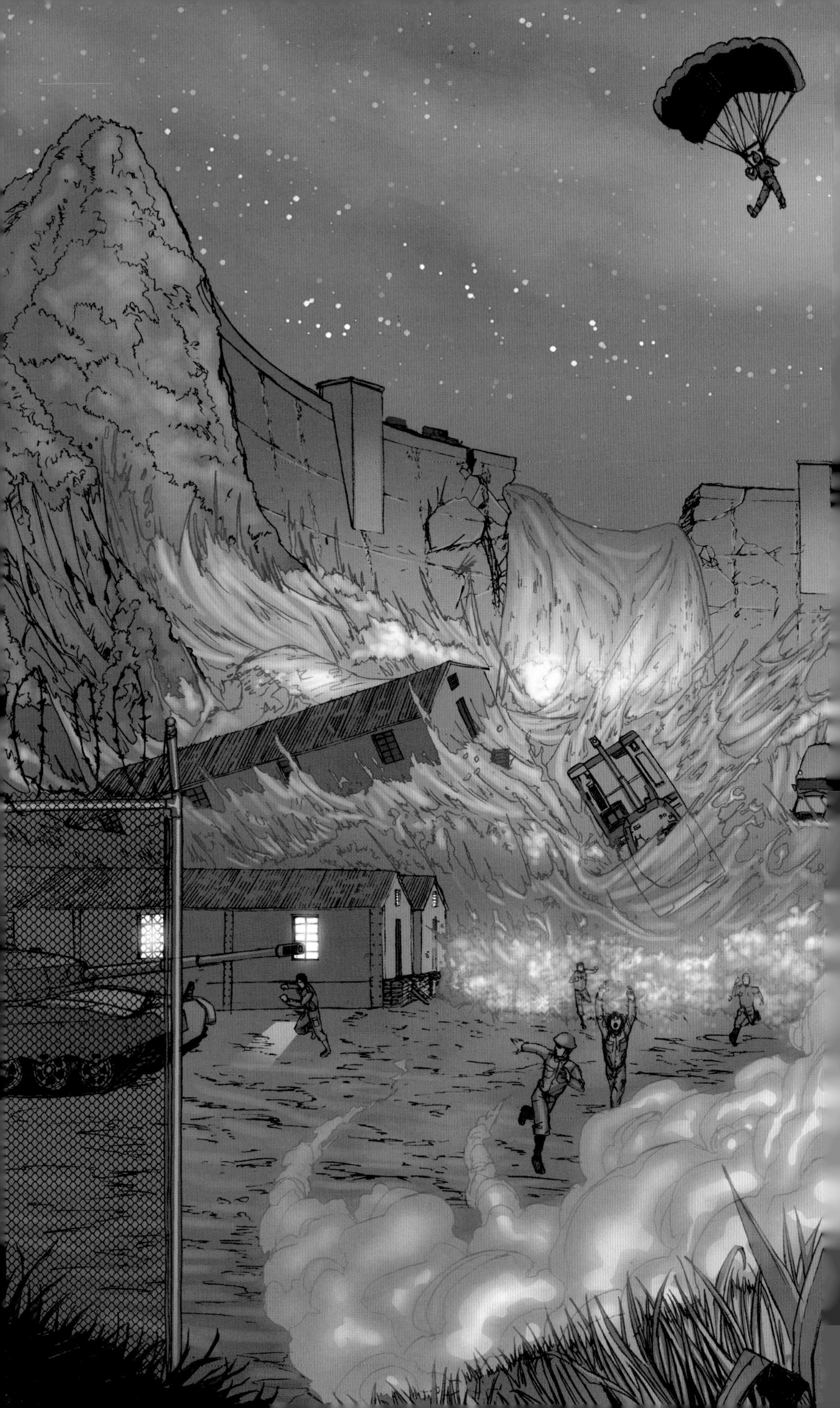

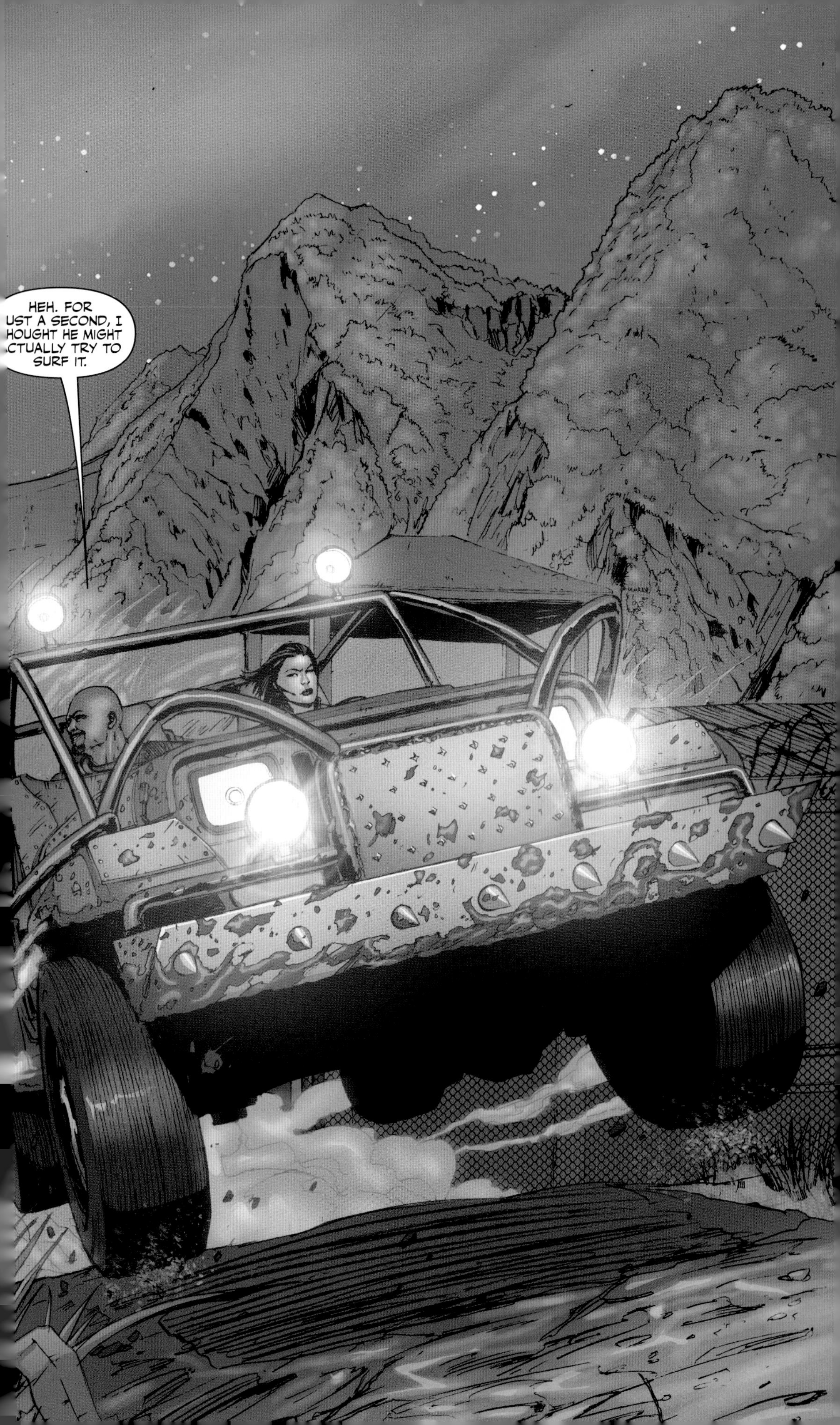
HEH. FOR UST A SECOND, I HOUGHT HE MIGHT CTUALLY TRY TO SURF IT.

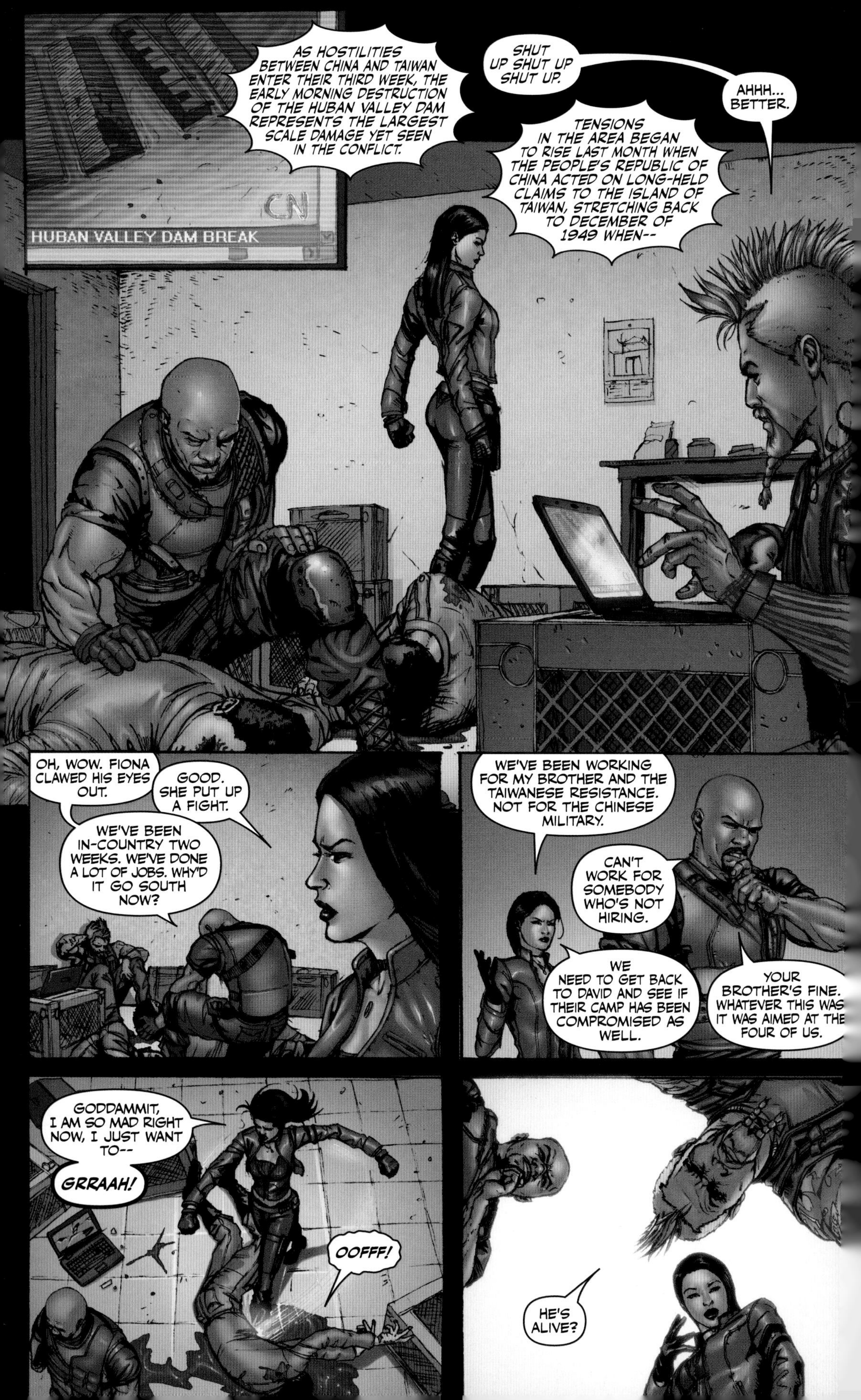

HUBAN VALLEY DAM BREAK
CN
AS HOSTILITIES BETWEEN CHINA AND TAIWAN ENTER THEIR THIRD WEEK, THE EARLY MORNING DESTRUCTION OF THE HUBAN VALLEY DAM REPRESENTS THE LARGEST SCALE DAMAGE YET SEEN IN THE CONFLICT.
SHUT UP SHUT UP SHUT UP.
AHHH... BETTER.
TENSIONS IN THE AREA BEGAN TO RISE LAST MONTH WHEN THE PEOPLE'S REPUBLIC OF CHINA ACTED ON LONG-HELD CLAIMS TO THE ISLAND OF TAIWAN, STRETCHING BACK TO DECEMBER OF 1949 WHEN--
OH, WOW. FIONA CLAWED HIS EYES OUT.
GOOD. SHE PUT UP A FIGHT.
WE'VE BEEN IN-COUNTRY TWO WEEKS. WE'VE DONE A LOT OF JOBS. WHY'D IT GO SOUTH NOW?
WE'VE BEEN WORKING FOR MY BROTHER AND THE TAIWANESE RESISTANCE. NOT FOR THE CHINESE MILITARY.
CAN'T WORK FOR SOMEBODY WHO'S NOT HIRING.
WE NEED TO GET BACK TO DAVID AND SEE IF THEIR CAMP HAS BEEN COMPROMISED AS WELL.
YOUR BROTHER'S FINE. WHATEVER THIS WAS IT WAS AIMED AT THE FOUR OF US.
GODDAMMIT, I AM SO MAD RIGHT NOW, I JUST WANT TO--
GRRAAH!
OOFFF!
HE'S ALIVE?

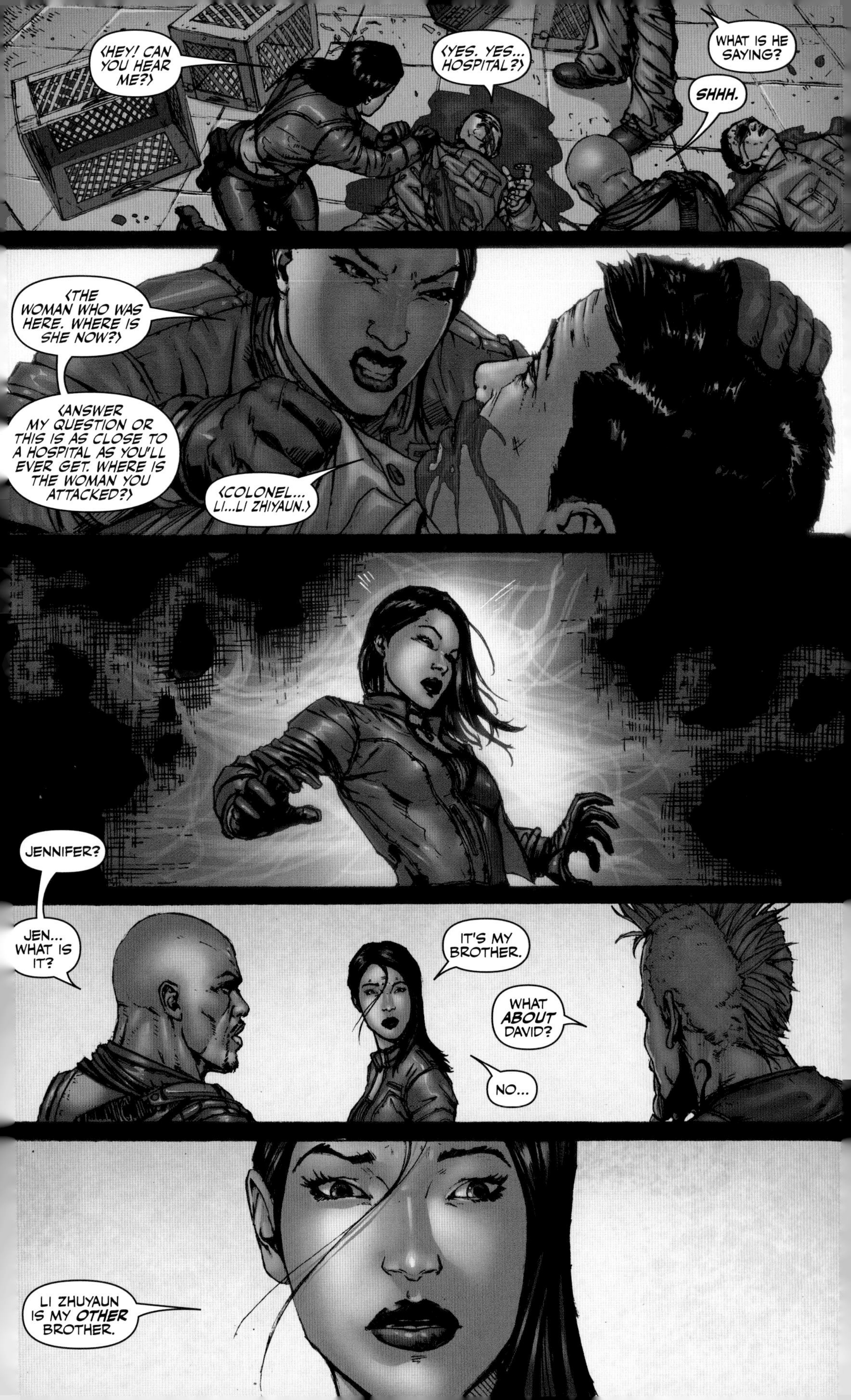

<HEY! CAN YOU HEAR ME?>
<YES. YES... HOSPITAL?>
WHAT IS HE SAYING?
SHHH.
<THE WOMAN WHO WAS HERE. WHERE IS SHE NOW?>
<ANSWER MY QUESTION OR THIS IS AS CLOSE TO A HOSPITAL AS YOU'LL EVER GET. WHERE IS THE WOMAN YOU ATTACKED?>
<COLONEL... LI...LI ZHIYAUN.>
JENNIFER?
JEN... WHAT IS IT?
IT'S MY BROTHER.
WHAT ABOUT DAVID?
NO...
LI ZHUYAUN IS MY OTHER BROTHER.

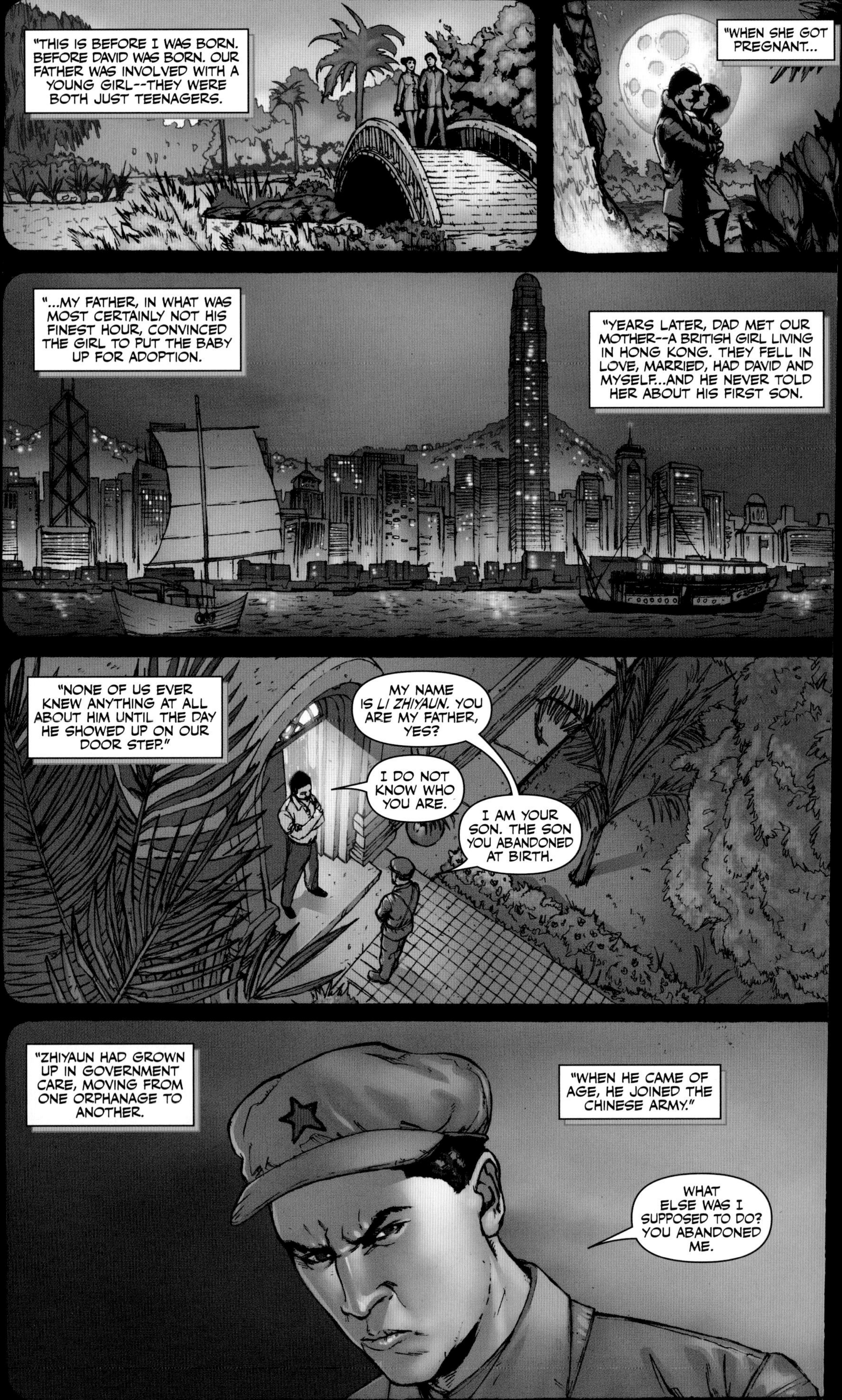
"THIS IS BEFORE I WAS BORN. BEFORE DAVID WAS BORN. OUR FATHER WAS INVOLVED WITH A YOUNG GIRL--THEY WERE BOTH JUST TEENAGERS.
"WHEN SHE GOT PREGNANT...
"...MY FATHER, IN WHAT WAS MOST CERTAINLY NOT HIS FINEST HOUR, CONVINCED THE GIRL TO PUT THE BABY UP FOR ADOPTION.
"YEARS LATER, DAD MET OUR MOTHER--A BRITISH GIRL LIVING IN HONG KONG. THEY FELL IN LOVE, MARRIED, HAD DAVID AND MYSELF...AND HE NEVER TOLD HER ABOUT HIS FIRST SON.
"NONE OF US EVER KNEW ANYTHING AT ALL ABOUT HIM UNTIL THE DAY HE SHOWED UP ON OUR DOOR STEP."
MY NAME IS *LI ZHIYAUN*. YOU ARE MY FATHER, YES?
I DO NOT KNOW WHO YOU ARE.
I AM YOUR SON. THE SON YOU ABANDONED AT BIRTH.
"ZHIYAUN HAD GROWN UP IN GOVERNMENT CARE, MOVING FROM ONE ORPHANAGE TO ANOTHER.
"WHEN HE CAME OF AGE, HE JOINED THE CHINESE ARMY."
WHAT ELSE WAS I SUPPOSED TO DO? YOU ABANDONED ME.

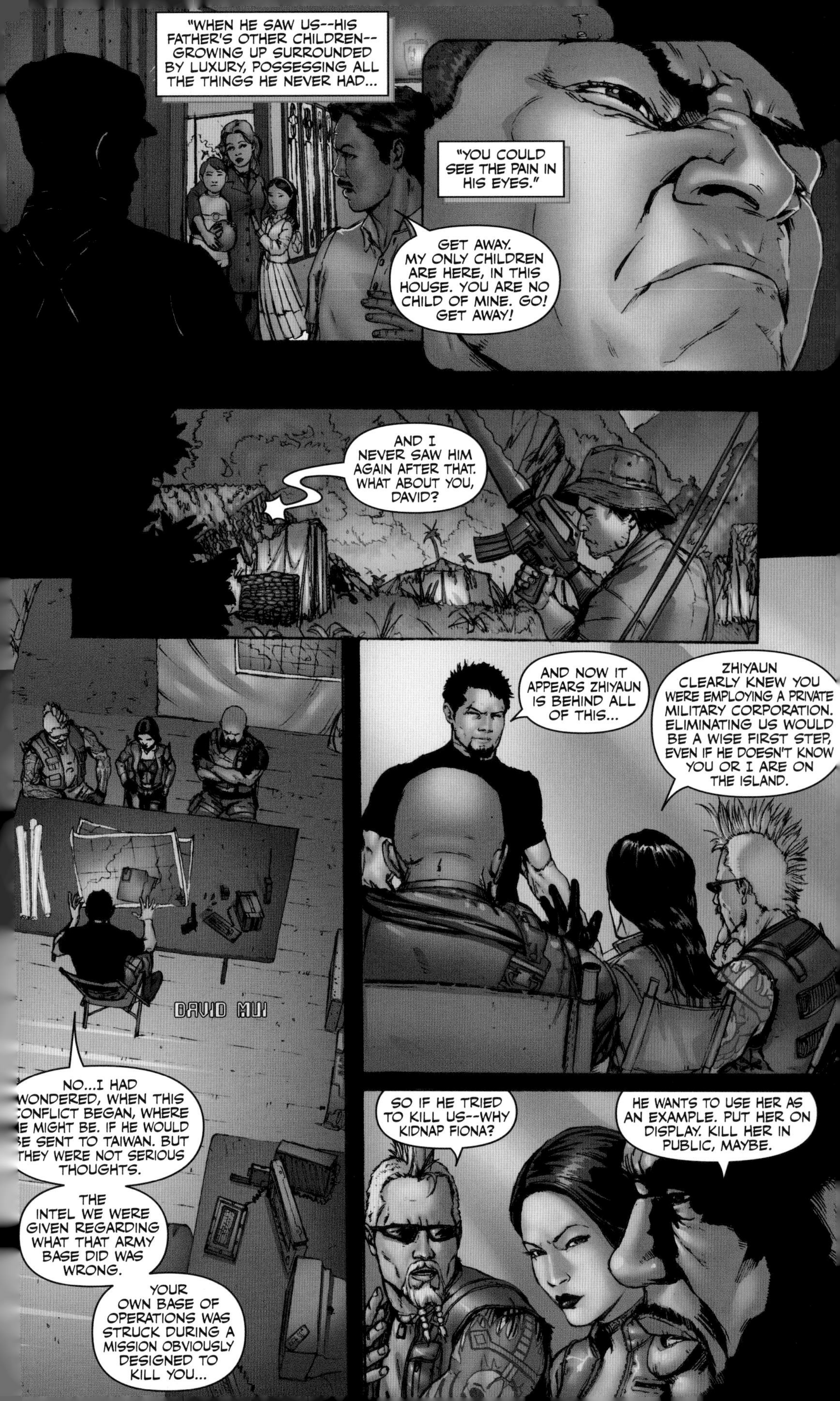
"WHEN HE SAW US--HIS FATHER'S OTHER CHILDREN--GROWING UP SURROUNDED BY LUXURY, POSSESSING ALL THE THINGS HE NEVER HAD...
GET AWAY. MY ONLY CHILDREN ARE HERE, IN THIS HOUSE. YOU ARE NO CHILD OF MINE. GO! GET AWAY!
"YOU COULD SEE THE PAIN IN HIS EYES."
AND I NEVER SAW HIM AGAIN AFTER THAT. WHAT ABOUT YOU, DAVID?
DAVID MUI
NO...I HAD WONDERED, WHEN THIS CONFLICT BEGAN, WHERE HE MIGHT BE. IF HE WOULD BE SENT TO TAIWAN. BUT THEY WERE NOT SERIOUS THOUGHTS.
THE INTEL WE WERE GIVEN REGARDING WHAT THAT ARMY BASE DID WAS WRONG.
YOUR OWN BASE OF OPERATIONS WAS STRUCK DURING A MISSION OBVIOUSLY DESIGNED TO KILL YOU...
AND NOW IT APPEARS ZHIYAUN IS BEHIND ALL OF THIS...
ZHIYAUN CLEARLY KNEW YOU WERE EMPLOYING A PRIVATE MILITARY CORPORATION. ELIMINATING US WOULD BE A WISE FIRST STEP, EVEN IF HE DOESN'T KNOW YOU OR I ARE ON THE ISLAND.
SO IF HE TRIED TO KILL US--WHY KIDNAP FIONA?
HE WANTS TO USE HER AS AN EXAMPLE. PUT HER ON DISPLAY. KILL HER IN PUBLIC, MAYBE.

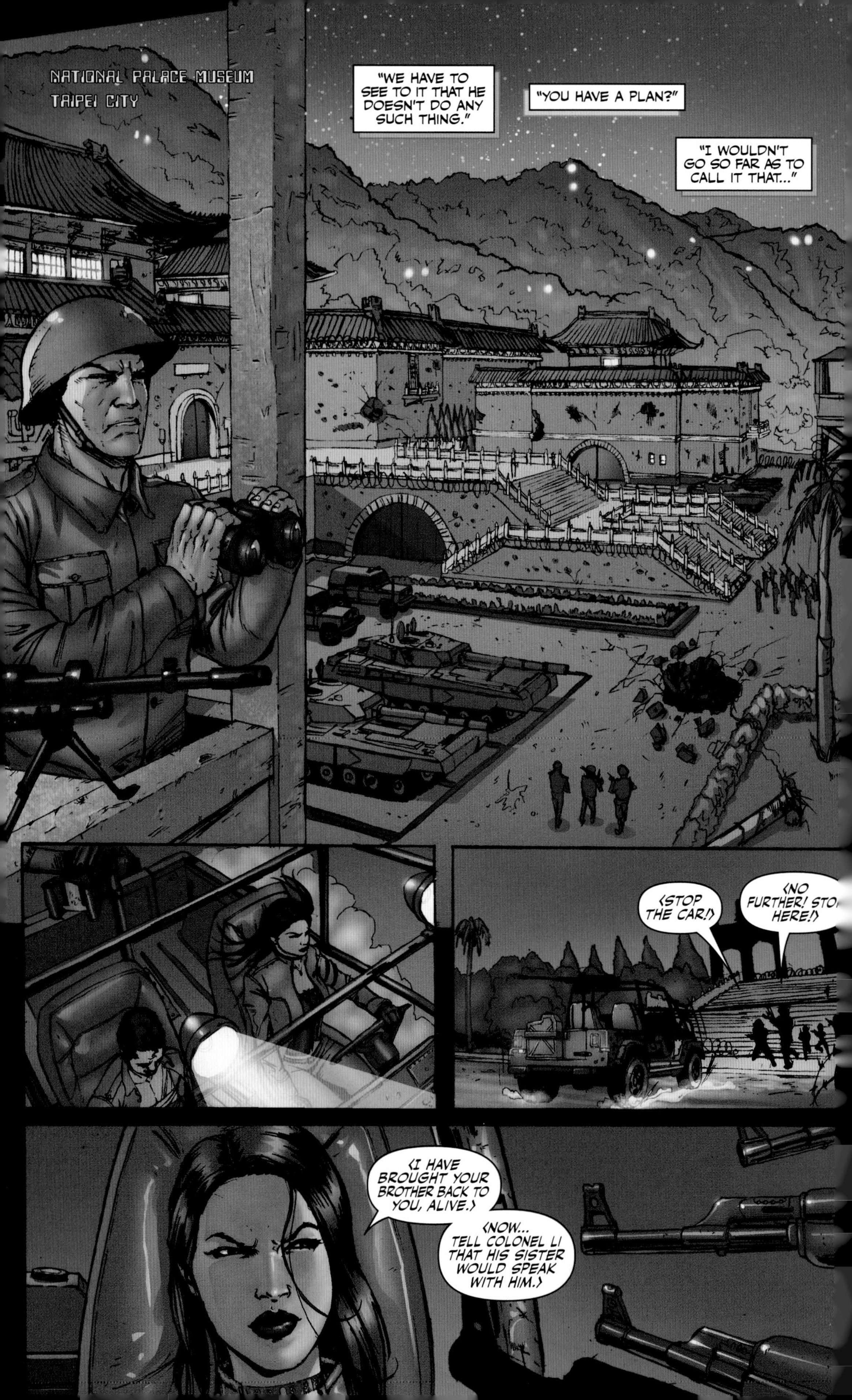
NATIONAL PALACE MUSEUM
TAIPEI CITY
"WE HAVE TO SEE TO IT THAT HE DOESN'T DO ANY SUCH THING."
"YOU HAVE A PLAN?"
"I WOULDN'T GO SO FAR AS TO CALL IT THAT..."
‹STOP THE CAR!›
‹NO FURTHER! STO HERE!›
‹I HAVE BROUGHT YOUR BROTHER BACK TO YOU, ALIVE.›
‹NOW... TELL COLONEL LI THAT HIS SISTER WOULD SPEAK WITH HIM.›

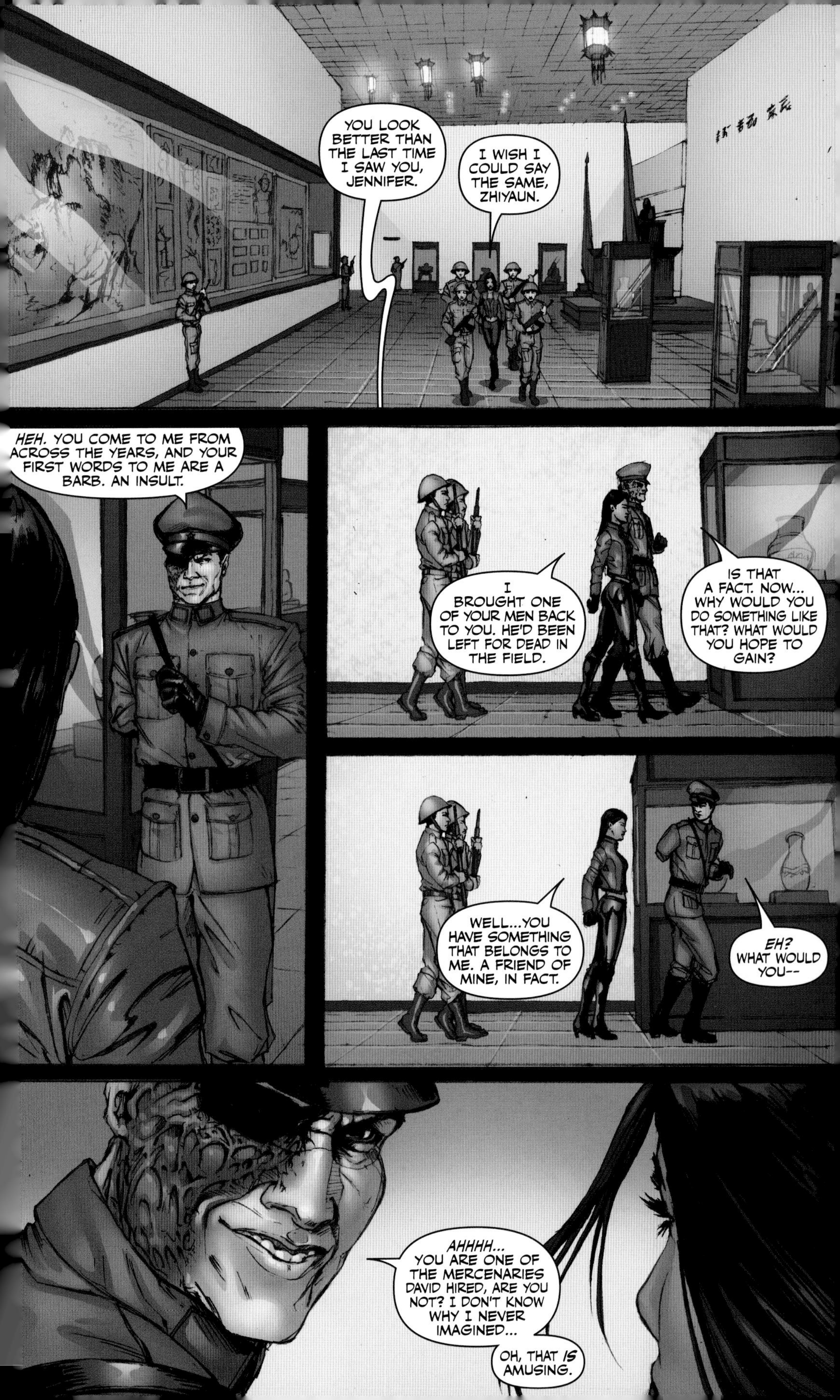
YOU LOOK BETTER THAN THE LAST TIME I SAW YOU, JENNIFER.
I WISH I COULD SAY THE SAME, ZHIYAUN.
HEH. YOU COME TO ME FROM ACROSS THE YEARS, AND YOUR FIRST WORDS TO ME ARE A BARB. AN INSULT.
I BROUGHT ONE OF YOUR MEN BACK TO YOU. HE'D BEEN LEFT FOR DEAD IN THE FIELD.
IS THAT A FACT. NOW... WHY WOULD YOU DO SOMETHING LIKE THAT? WHAT WOULD YOU HOPE TO GAIN?
WELL...YOU HAVE SOMETHING THAT BELONGS TO ME. A FRIEND OF MINE, IN FACT.
EH? WHAT WOULD YOU--
AHHHH... YOU ARE ONE OF THE MERCENARIES DAVID HIRED, ARE YOU NOT? I DON'T KNOW WHY I NEVER IMAGINED...
OH, THAT *IS* AMUSING.

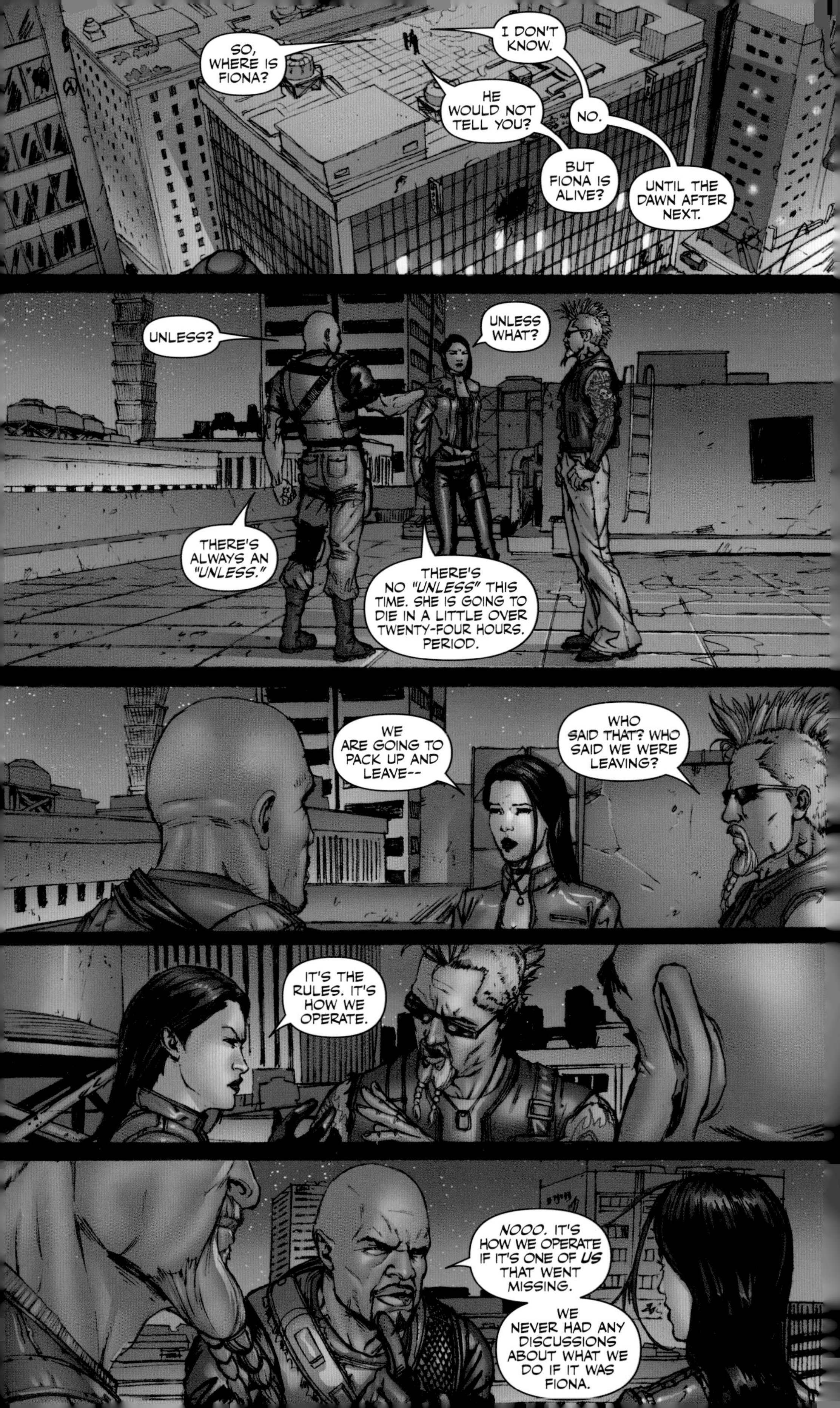
SO, WHERE IS FIONA?
I DON'T KNOW.
HE WOULD NOT TELL YOU?
NO.
BUT FIONA IS ALIVE?
UNTIL THE DAWN AFTER NEXT.
UNLESS?
UNLESS WHAT?
THERE'S ALWAYS AN "UNLESS."
THERE'S NO "UNLESS" THIS TIME. SHE IS GOING TO DIE IN A LITTLE OVER TWENTY-FOUR HOURS. PERIOD.
WE ARE GOING TO PACK UP AND LEAVE--
WHO SAID THAT? WHO SAID WE WERE LEAVING?
IT'S THE RULES. IT'S HOW WE OPERATE.
NOOO. IT'S HOW WE OPERATE IF IT'S ONE OF US THAT WENT MISSING.
WE NEVER HAD ANY DISCUSSIONS ABOUT WHAT WE DO IF IT WAS FIONA.

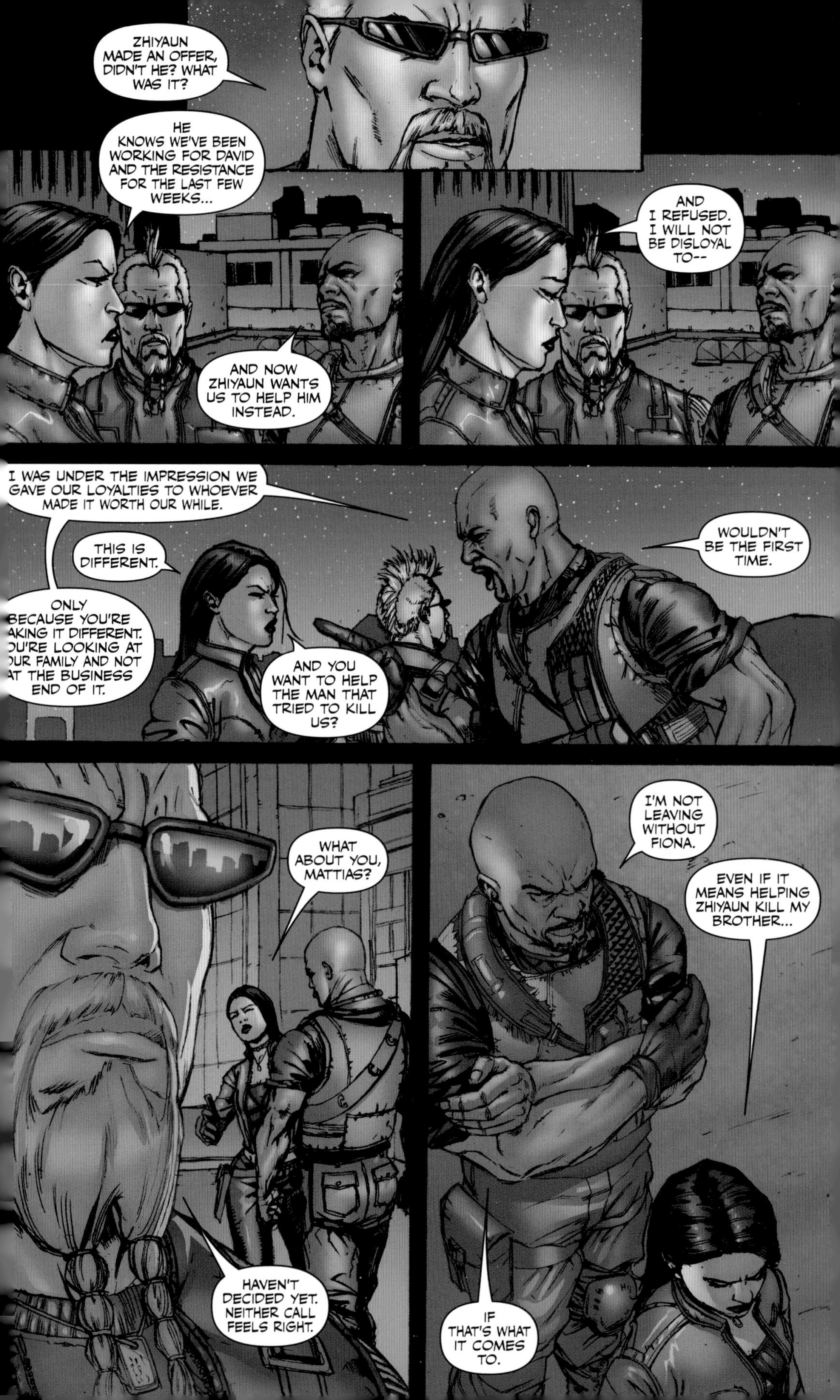

ZHIYAUN MADE AN OFFER, DIDN'T HE? WHAT WAS IT?
HE KNOWS WE'VE BEEN WORKING FOR DAVID AND THE RESISTANCE FOR THE LAST FEW WEEKS...
AND NOW ZHIYAUN WANTS US TO HELP HIM INSTEAD.
AND I REFUSED. I WILL NOT BE DISLOYAL TO--
I WAS UNDER THE IMPRESSION WE GAVE OUR LOYALTIES TO WHOEVER MADE IT WORTH OUR WHILE.
THIS IS DIFFERENT.
ONLY BECAUSE YOU'RE AKING IT DIFFERENT. OU'RE LOOKING AT OUR FAMILY AND NOT AT THE BUSINESS END OF IT.
AND YOU WANT TO HELP THE MAN THAT TRIED TO KILL US?
WOULDN'T BE THE FIRST TIME.
WHAT ABOUT YOU, MATTIAS?
HAVEN'T DECIDED YET. NEITHER CALL FEELS RIGHT.
I'M NOT LEAVING WITHOUT FIONA.
EVEN IF IT MEANS HELPING ZHIYAUN KILL MY BROTHER...
IF THAT'S WHAT IT COMES TO.

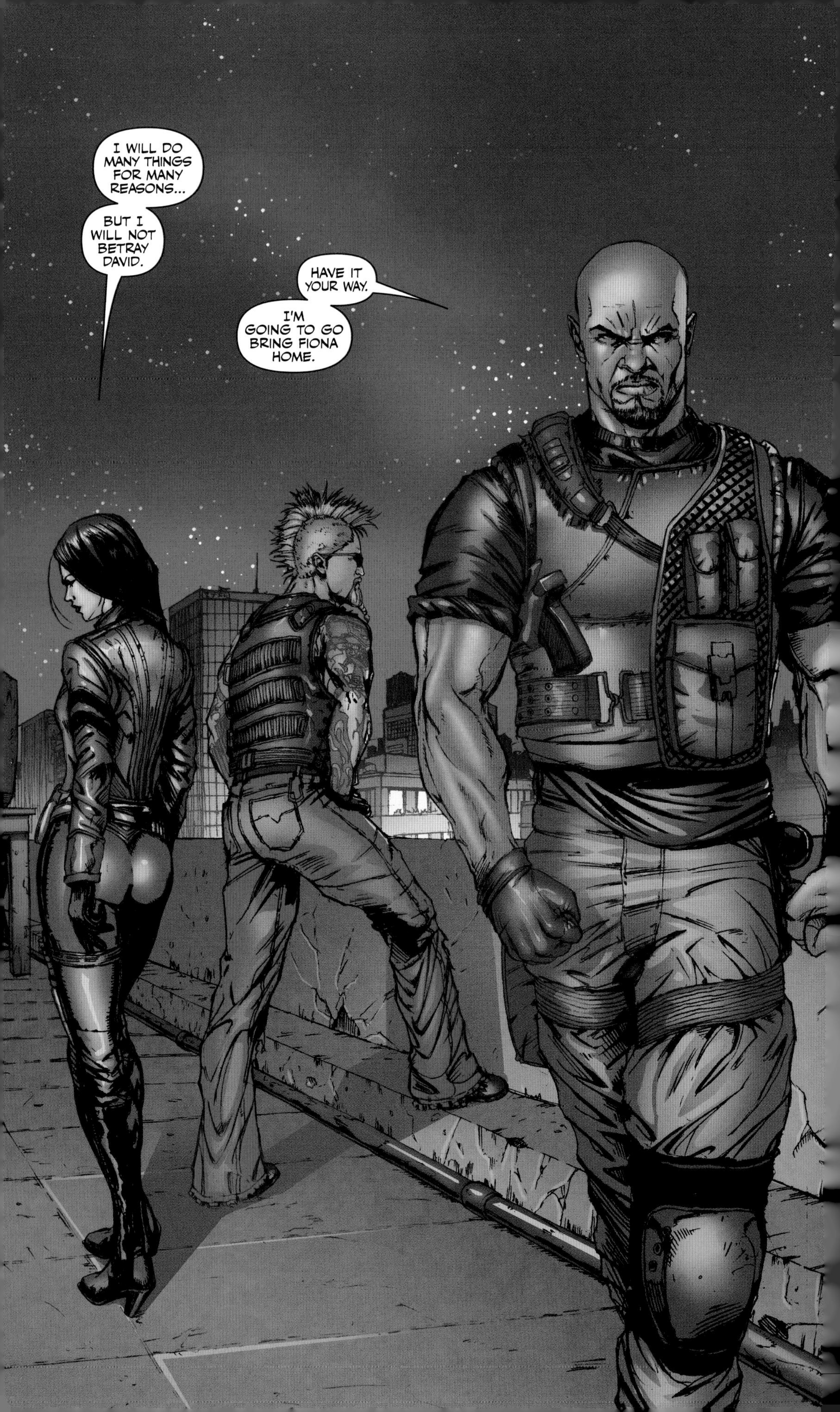
I WILL DO MANY THINGS FOR MANY REASONS...
BUT I WILL NOT BETRAY DAVID.
HAVE IT YOUR WAY.
I'M GOING TO GO BRING FIONA HOME.

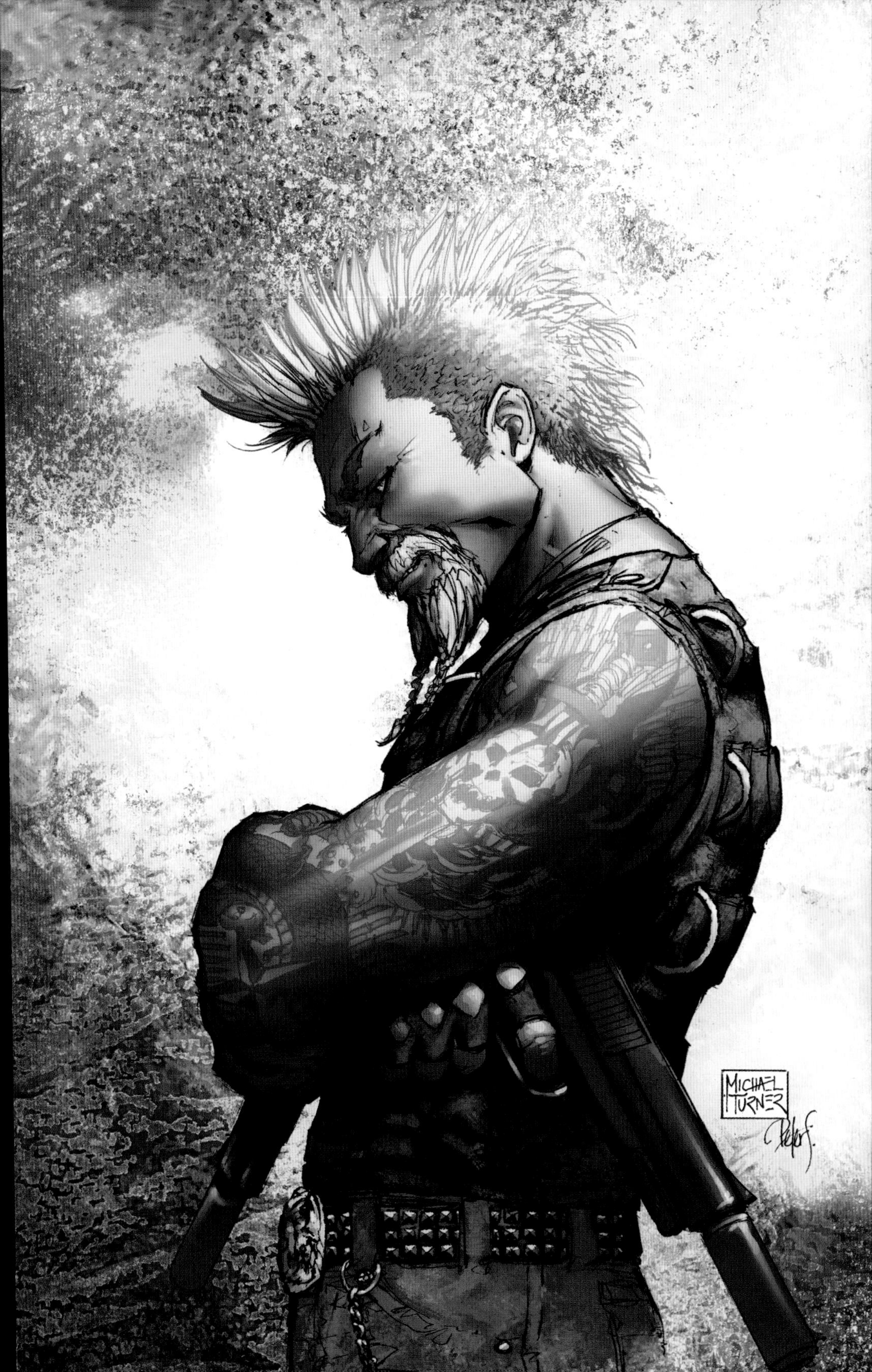
MICHAEL TURNER

CHAPTER TWO

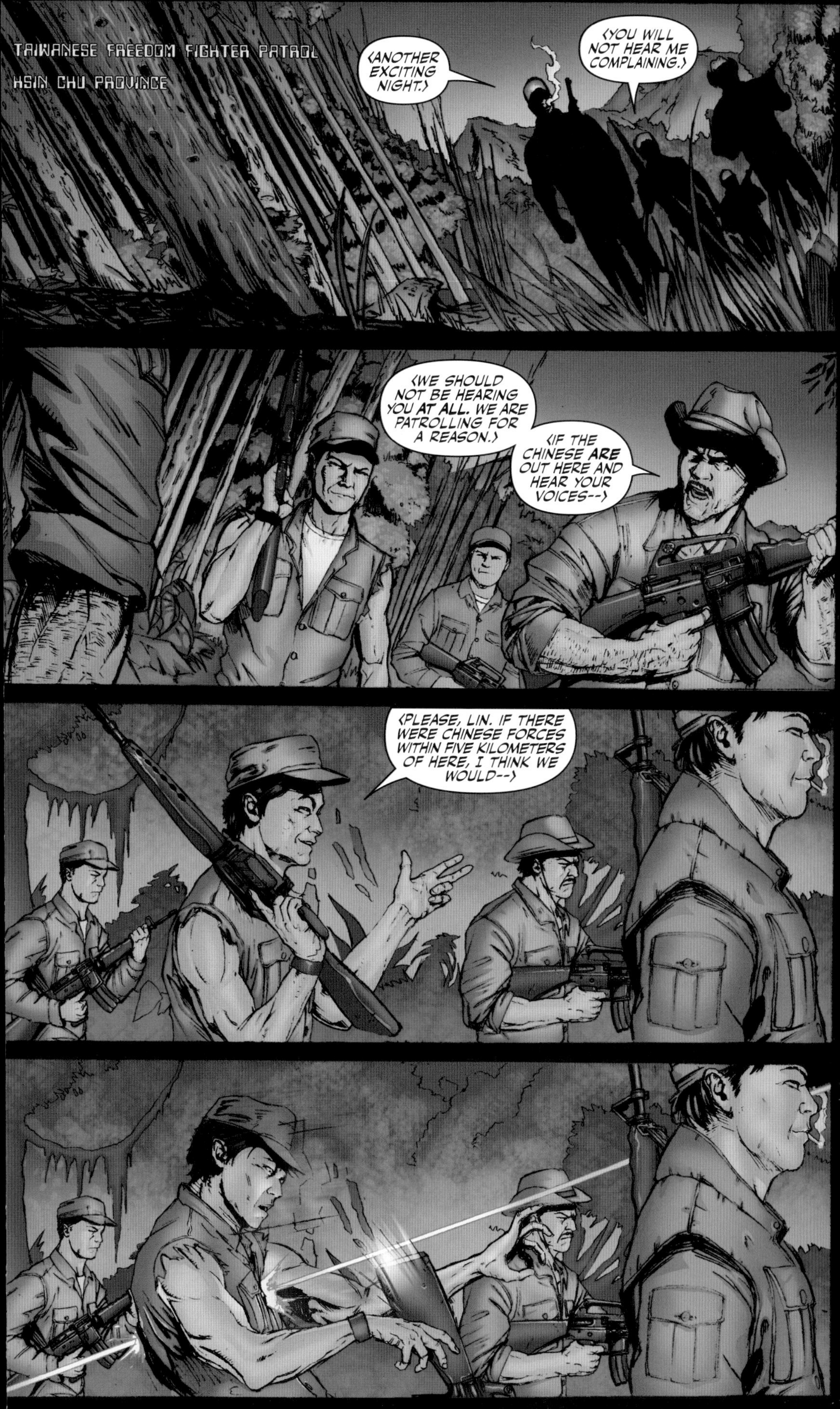

TAIWANESE FREEDOM FIGHTER PATROL
HSIN CHU PROVINCE
‹ANOTHER EXCITING NIGHT.›
‹YOU WILL NOT HEAR ME COMPLAINING.›
‹WE SHOULD NOT BE HEARING YOU AT ALL. WE ARE PATROLLING FOR A REASON.›
‹IF THE CHINESE ARE OUT HERE AND HEAR YOUR VOICES--›
‹PLEASE, LIN. IF THERE WERE CHINESE FORCES WITHIN FIVE KILOMETERS OF HERE, I THINK WE WOULD--›

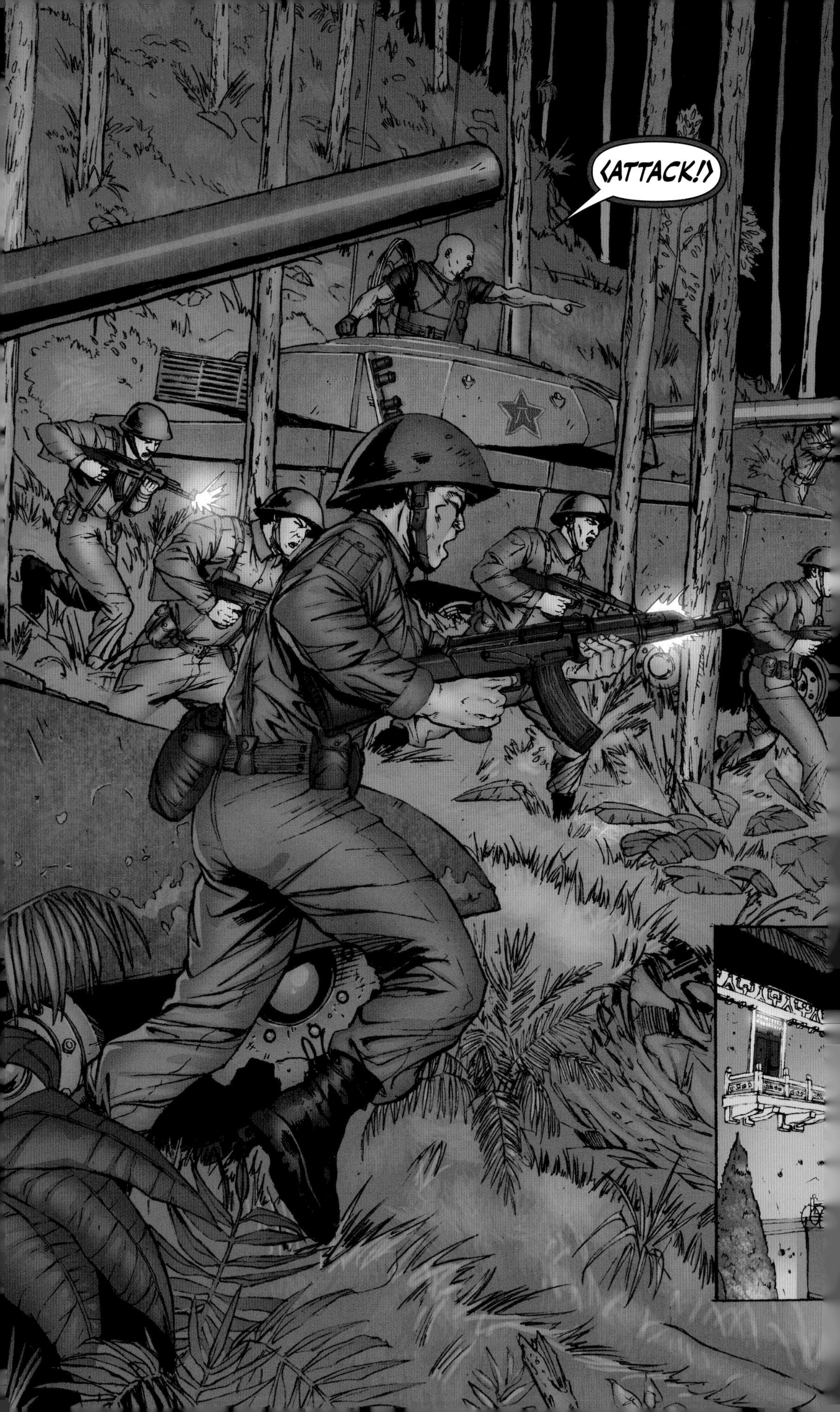
‹ATTACK!›

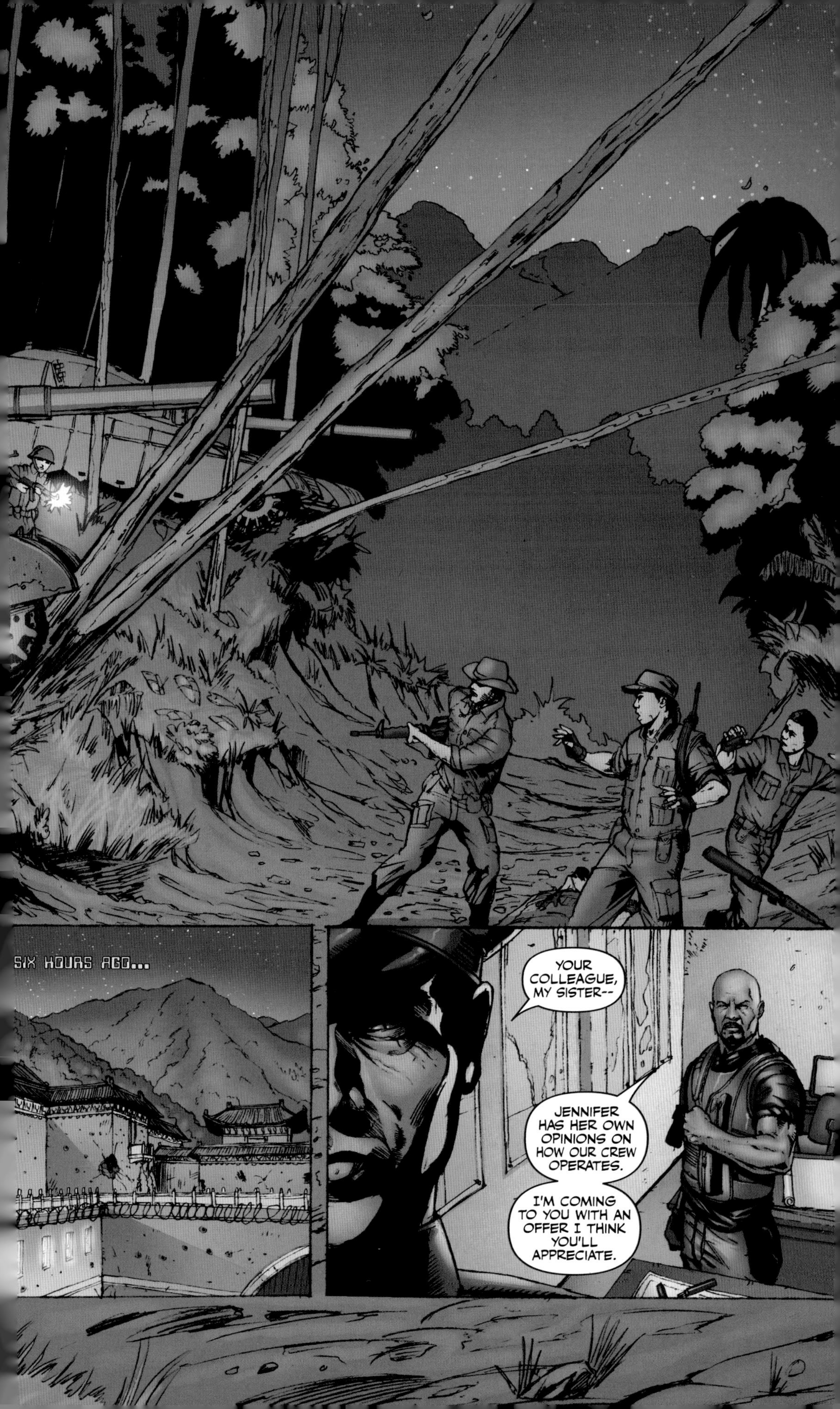

SIX HOURS AGO...
YOUR COLLEAGUE, MY SISTER--
JENNIFER HAS HER OWN OPINIONS ON HOW OUR CREW OPERATES.
I'M COMING TO YOU WITH AN OFFER I THINK YOU'LL APPRECIATE.

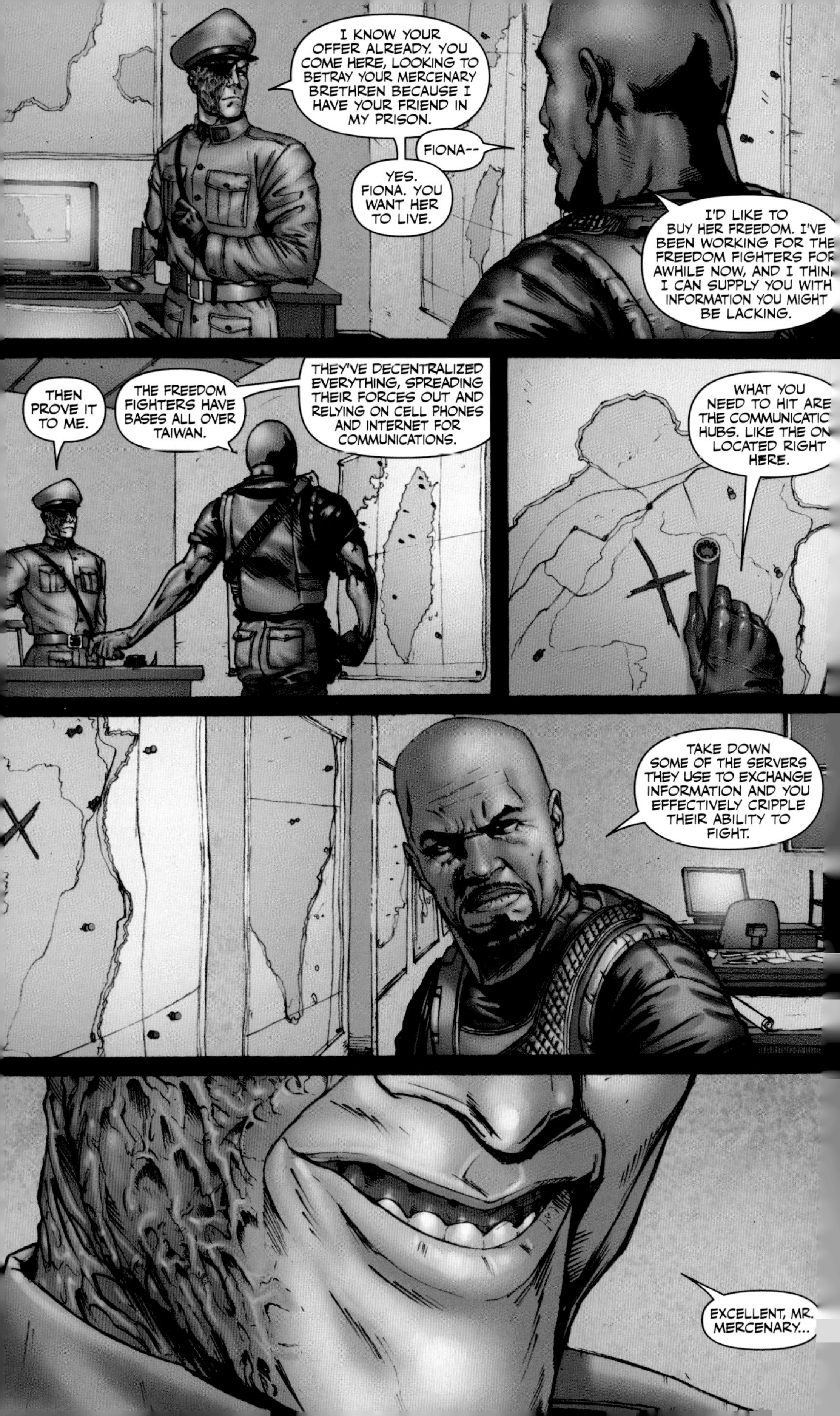
I KNOW YOUR OFFER ALREADY. YOU COME HERE, LOOKING TO BETRAY YOUR MERCENARY BRETHREN BECAUSE I HAVE YOUR FRIEND IN MY PRISON.
FIONA--
YES. FIONA. YOU WANT HER TO LIVE.
I'D LIKE TO BUY HER FREEDOM. I'VE BEEN WORKING FOR THE FREEDOM FIGHTERS FOR AWHILE NOW, AND I THIN I CAN SUPPLY YOU WITH INFORMATION YOU MIGHT BE LACKING.
THEN PROVE IT TO ME.
THE FREEDOM FIGHTERS HAVE BASES ALL OVER TAIWAN.
THEY'VE DECENTRALIZED EVERYTHING, SPREADING THEIR FORCES OUT AND RELYING ON CELL PHONES AND INTERNET FOR COMMUNICATIONS.
WHAT YOU NEED TO HIT ARE THE COMMUNICATIC HUBS. LIKE THE ON LOCATED RIGHT HERE.
TAKE DOWN SOME OF THE SERVERS THEY USE TO EXCHANGE INFORMATION AND YOU EFFECTIVELY CRIPPLE THEIR ABILITY TO FIGHT.
EXCELLENT, MR. MERCENARY...

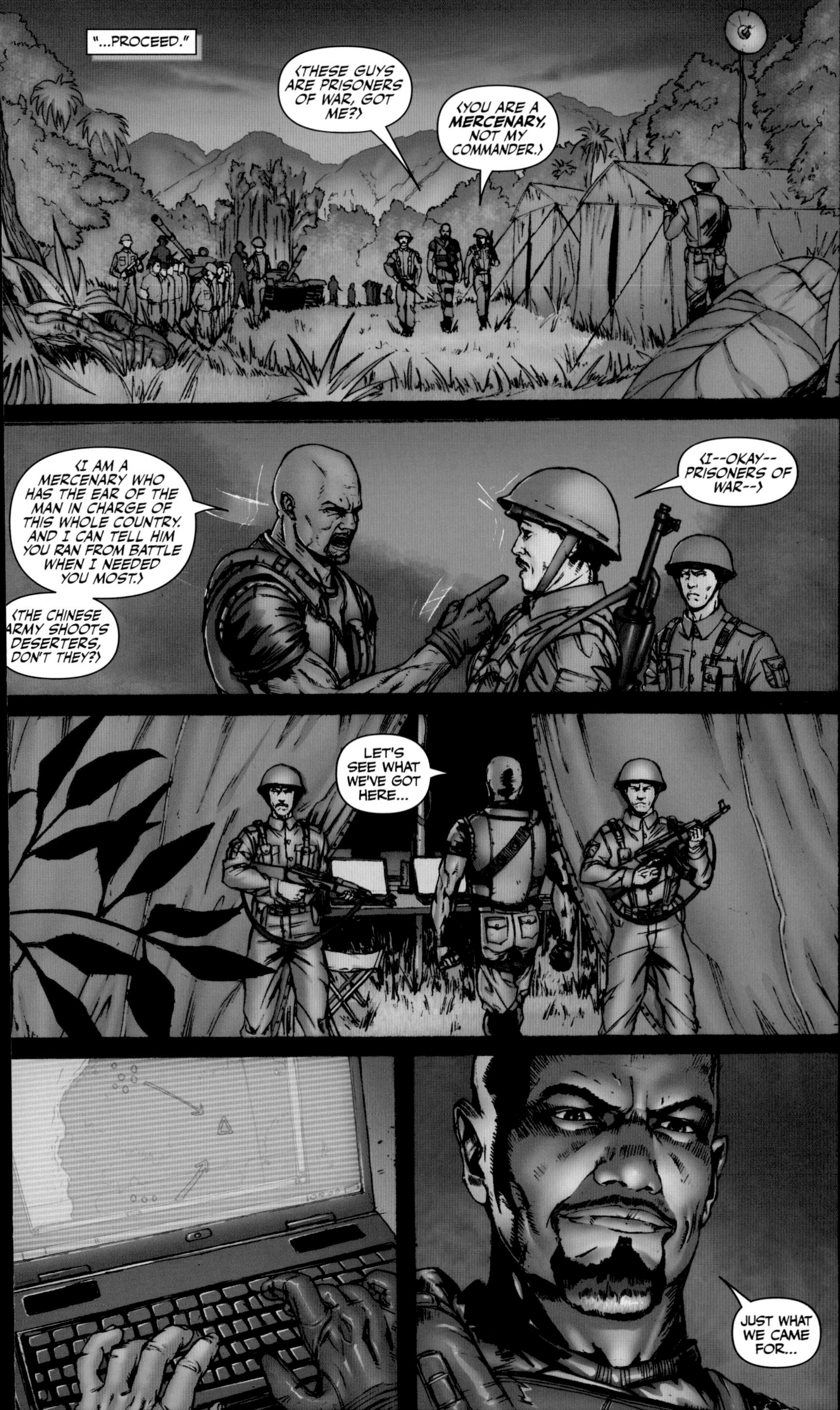
"...PROCEED."
‹THESE GUYS ARE PRISONERS OF WAR, GOT ME?›
‹YOU ARE A MERCENARY, NOT MY COMMANDER.›
‹I AM A MERCENARY WHO HAS THE EAR OF THE MAN IN CHARGE OF THIS WHOLE COUNTRY. AND I CAN TELL HIM YOU RAN FROM BATTLE WHEN I NEEDED YOU MOST.›
‹THE CHINESE ARMY SHOOTS DESERTERS, DON'T THEY?›
‹I--OKAY-- PRISONERS OF WAR--›
LET'S SEE WHAT WE'VE GOT HERE...
JUST WHAT WE CAME FOR...

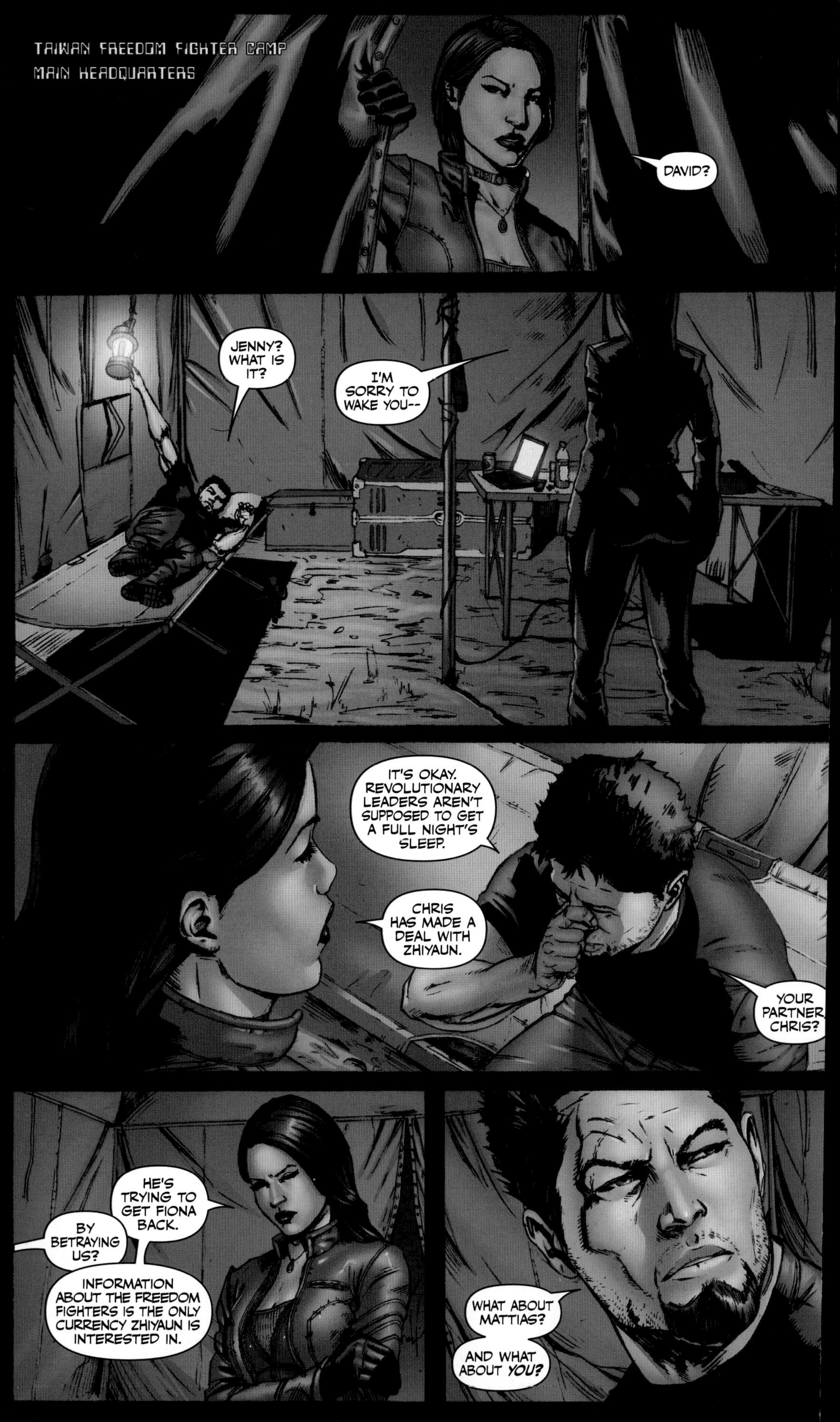
TAIWAN FREEDOM FIGHTER CAMP
MAIN HEADQUARTERS
DAVID?
JENNY? WHAT IS IT?
I'M SORRY TO WAKE YOU--
IT'S OKAY. REVOLUTIONARY LEADERS AREN'T SUPPOSED TO GET A FULL NIGHT'S SLEEP.
CHRIS HAS MADE A DEAL WITH ZHIYAUN.
YOUR PARTNER, CHRIS?
HE'S TRYING TO GET FIONA BACK.
BY BETRAYING US?
INFORMATION ABOUT THE FREEDOM FIGHTERS IS THE ONLY CURRENCY ZHIYAUN IS INTERESTED IN.
WHAT ABOUT MATTIAS?
AND WHAT ABOUT YOU?

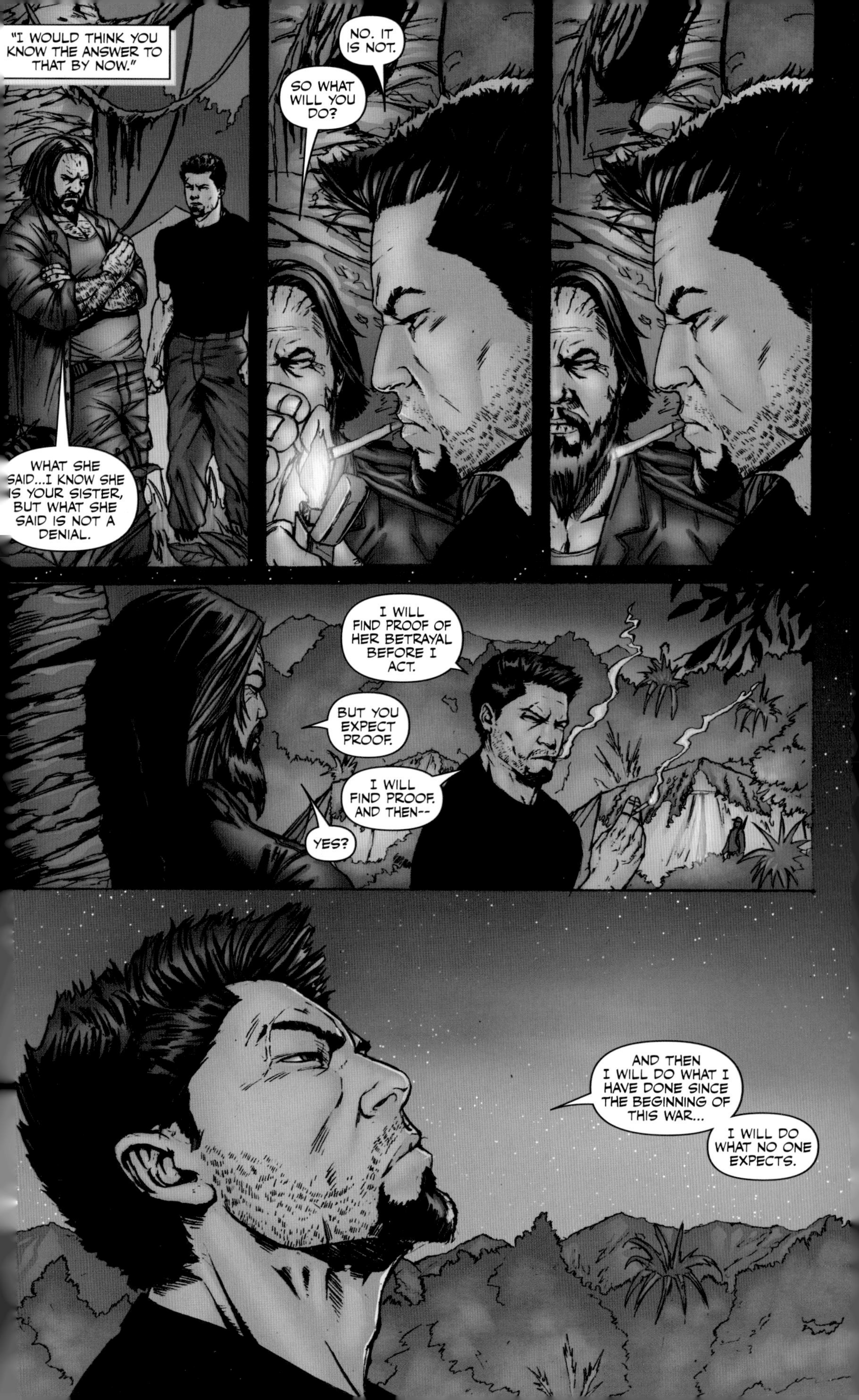
"I WOULD THINK YOU KNOW THE ANSWER TO THAT BY NOW."
WHAT SHE SAID...I KNOW SHE IS YOUR SISTER, BUT WHAT SHE SAID IS NOT A DENIAL.
NO. IT IS NOT.
SO WHAT WILL YOU DO?
I WILL FIND PROOF OF HER BETRAYAL BEFORE I ACT.
BUT YOU EXPECT PROOF.
I WILL FIND PROOF. AND THEN--
YES?
AND THEN I WILL DO WHAT I HAVE DONE SINCE THE BEGINNING OF THIS WAR...
I WILL DO WHAT NO ONE EXPECTS.

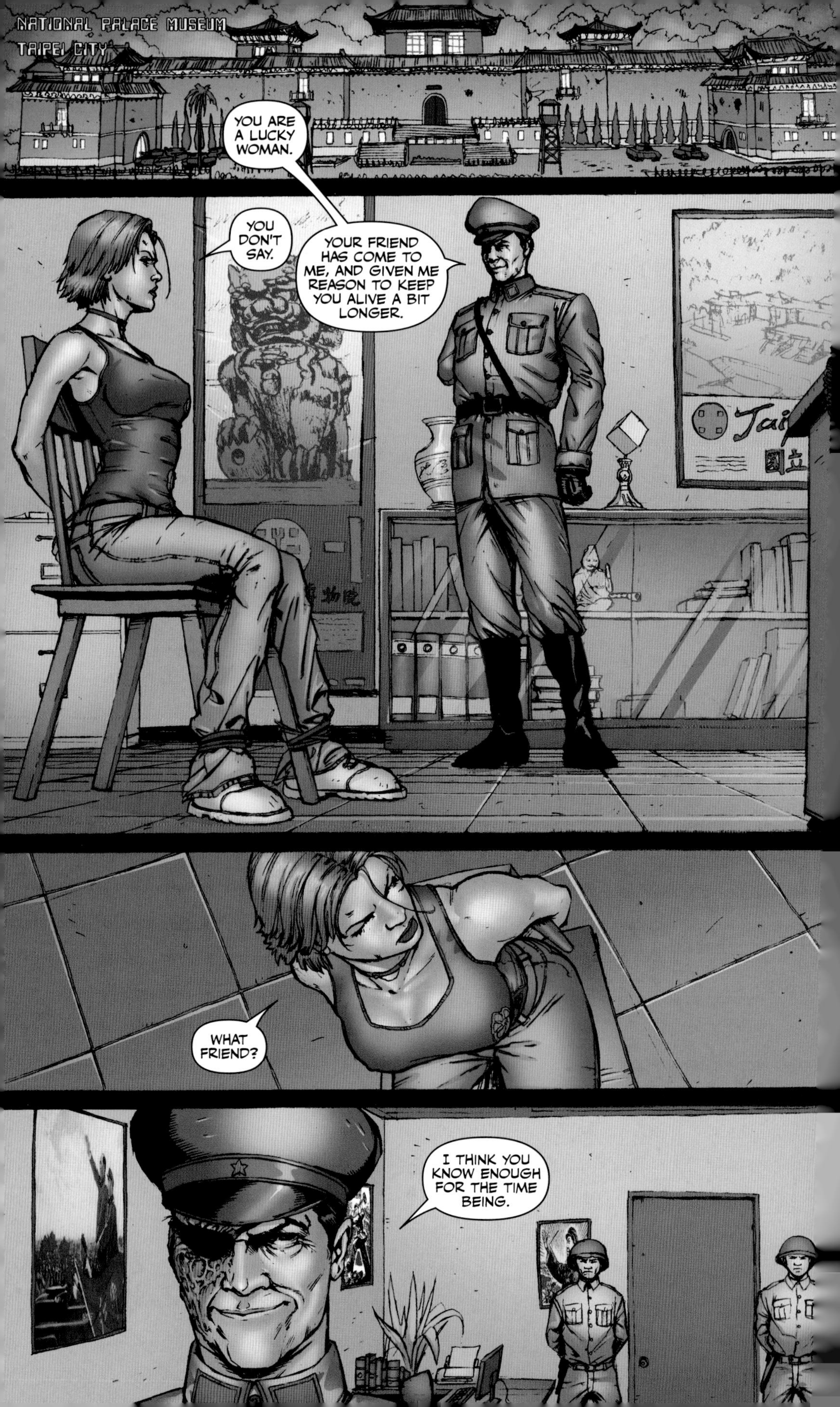
NATIONAL PALACE MUSEUM
TAIPEI CITY
YOU ARE A LUCKY WOMAN.
YOU DON'T SAY.
YOUR FRIEND HAS COME TO ME, AND GIVEN ME REASON TO KEEP YOU ALIVE A BIT LONGER.
WHAT FRIEND?
I THINK YOU KNOW ENOUGH FOR THE TIME BEING.

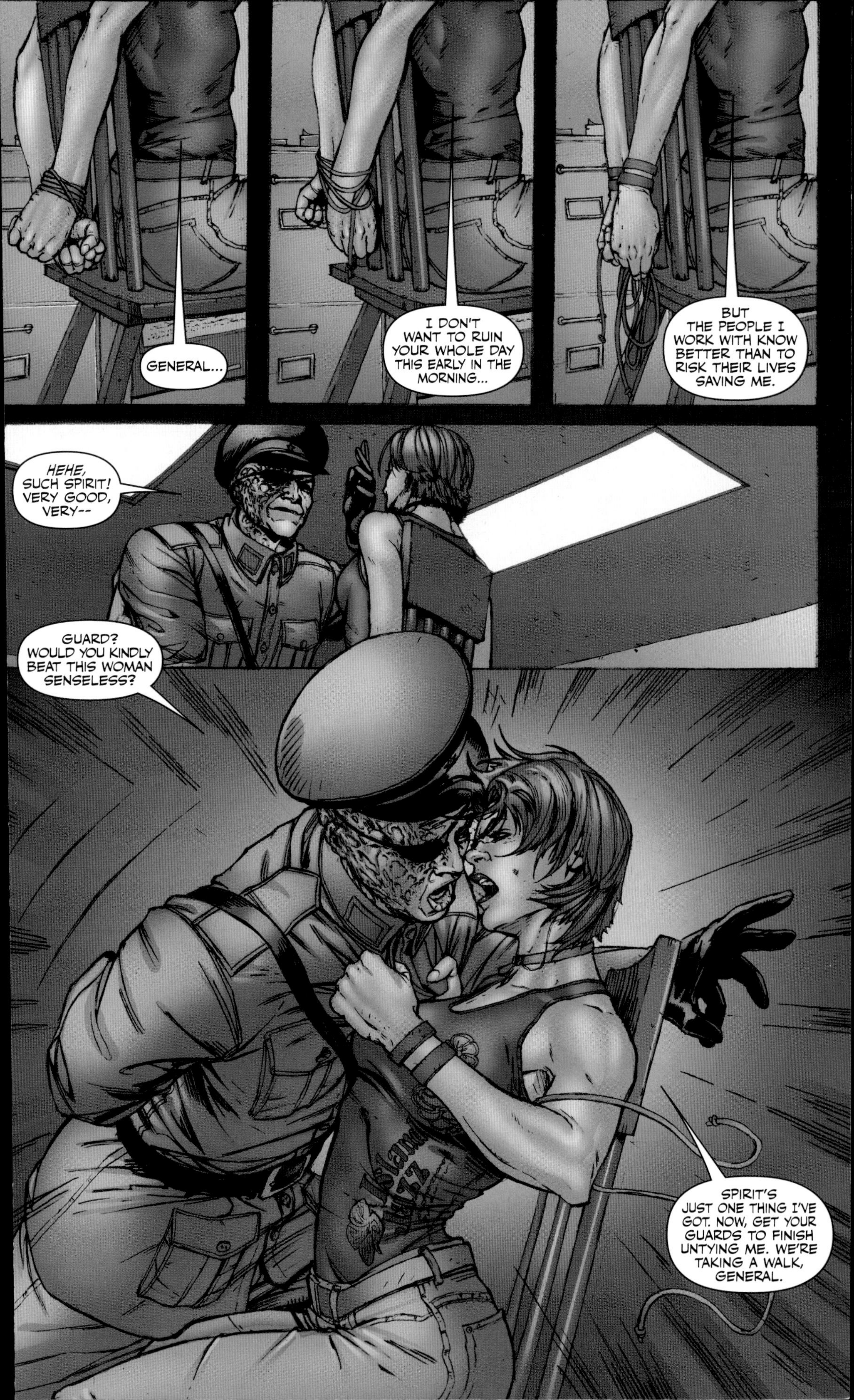
GENERAL...
I DON'T WANT TO RUIN YOUR WHOLE DAY THIS EARLY IN THE MORNING...
BUT THE PEOPLE I WORK WITH KNOW BETTER THAN TO RISK THEIR LIVES SAVING ME.
HEHE, SUCH SPIRIT! VERY GOOD, VERY--
GUARD? WOULD YOU KINDLY BEAT THIS WOMAN SENSELESS?
SPIRIT'S JUST ONE THING I'VE GOT. NOW, GET YOUR GUARDS TO FINISH UNTYING ME. WE'RE TAKING A WALK, GENERAL.

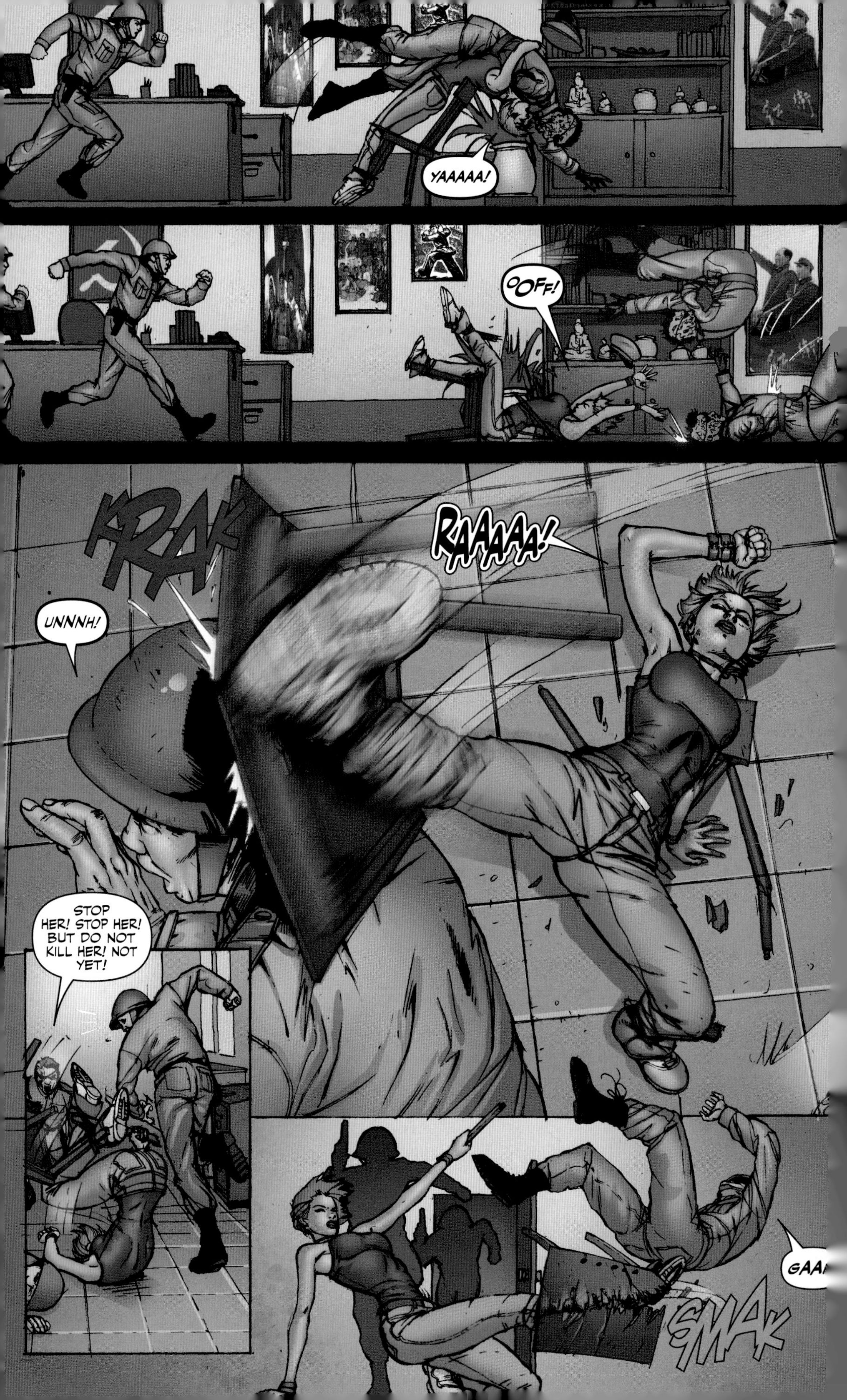
YAAAAA!
OOFF!
KRAK
RAAAAA!
UNNNH!
STOP HER! STOP HER! BUT DO NOT KILL HER! NOT YET!
SMAK

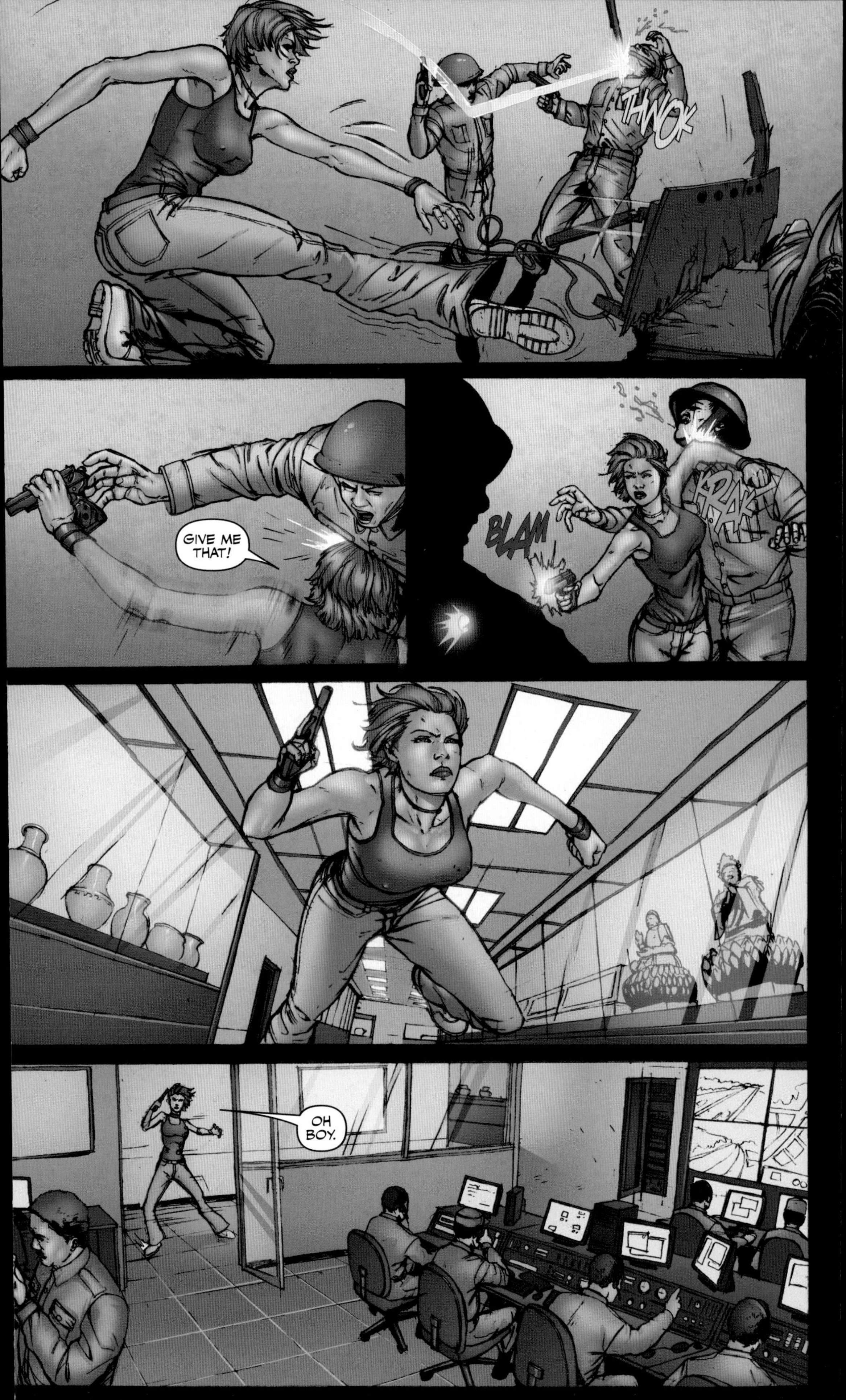
THWOK
GIVE ME THAT!
BLAM
KRAK
OH BOY.

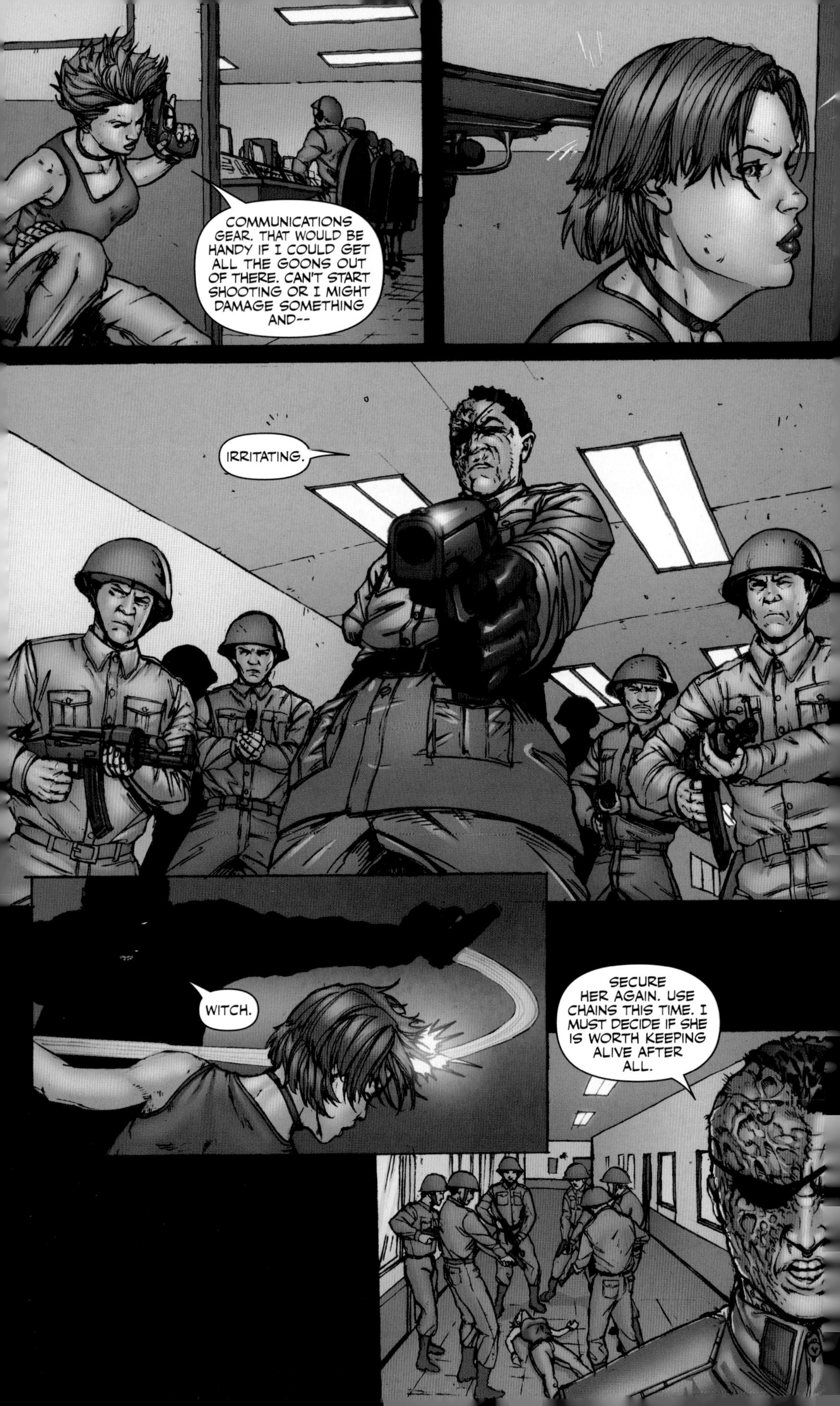
COMMUNICATIONS GEAR. THAT WOULD BE HANDY IF I COULD GET ALL THE GOONS OUT OF THERE. CAN'T START SHOOTING OR I MIGHT DAMAGE SOMETHING AND--
IRRITATING.
WITCH.
SECURE HER AGAIN. USE CHAINS THIS TIME. I MUST DECIDE IF SHE IS WORTH KEEPING ALIVE AFTER ALL.

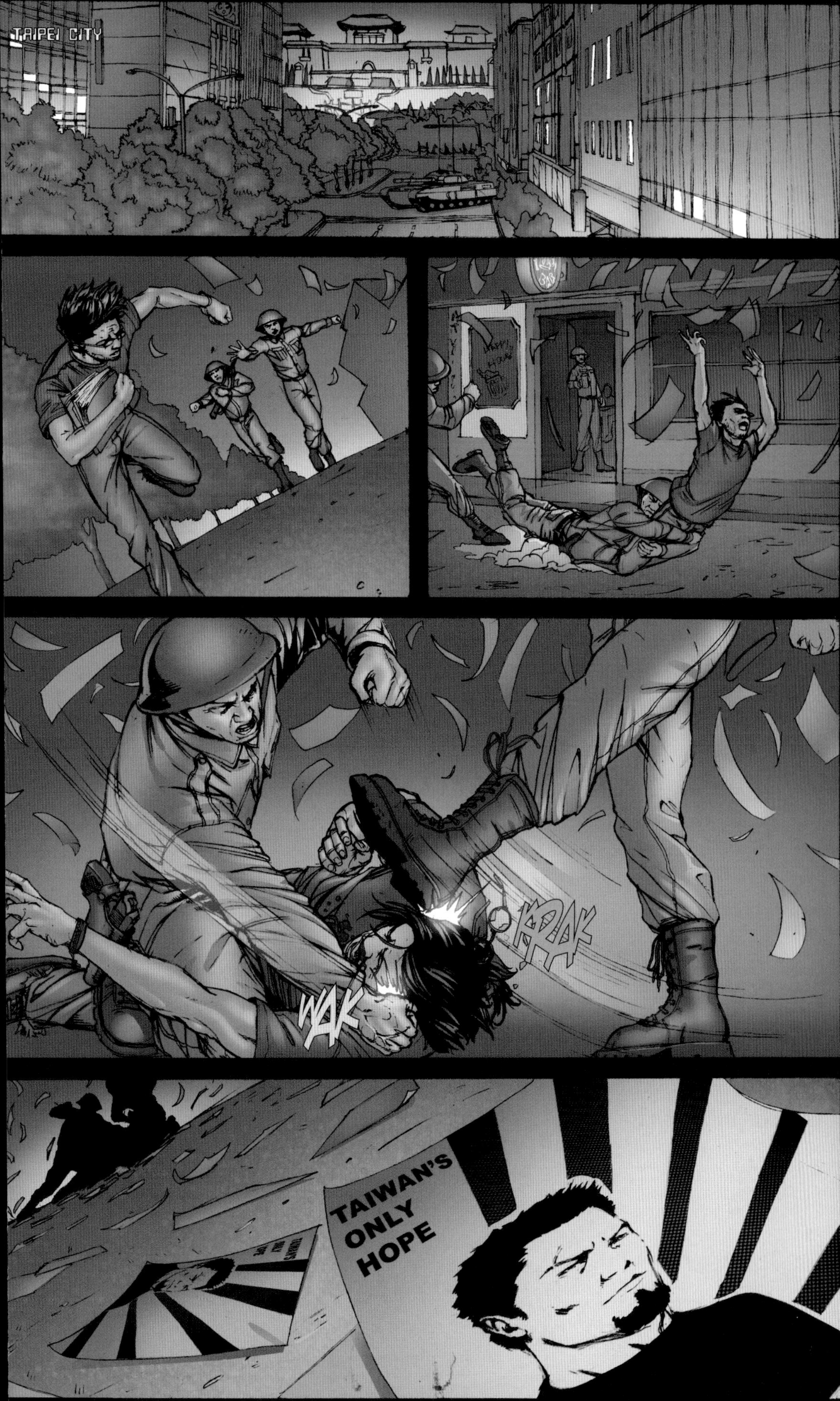
TAIPEI CITY
KRAK
WAK
TAIWAN'S ONLY HOPE

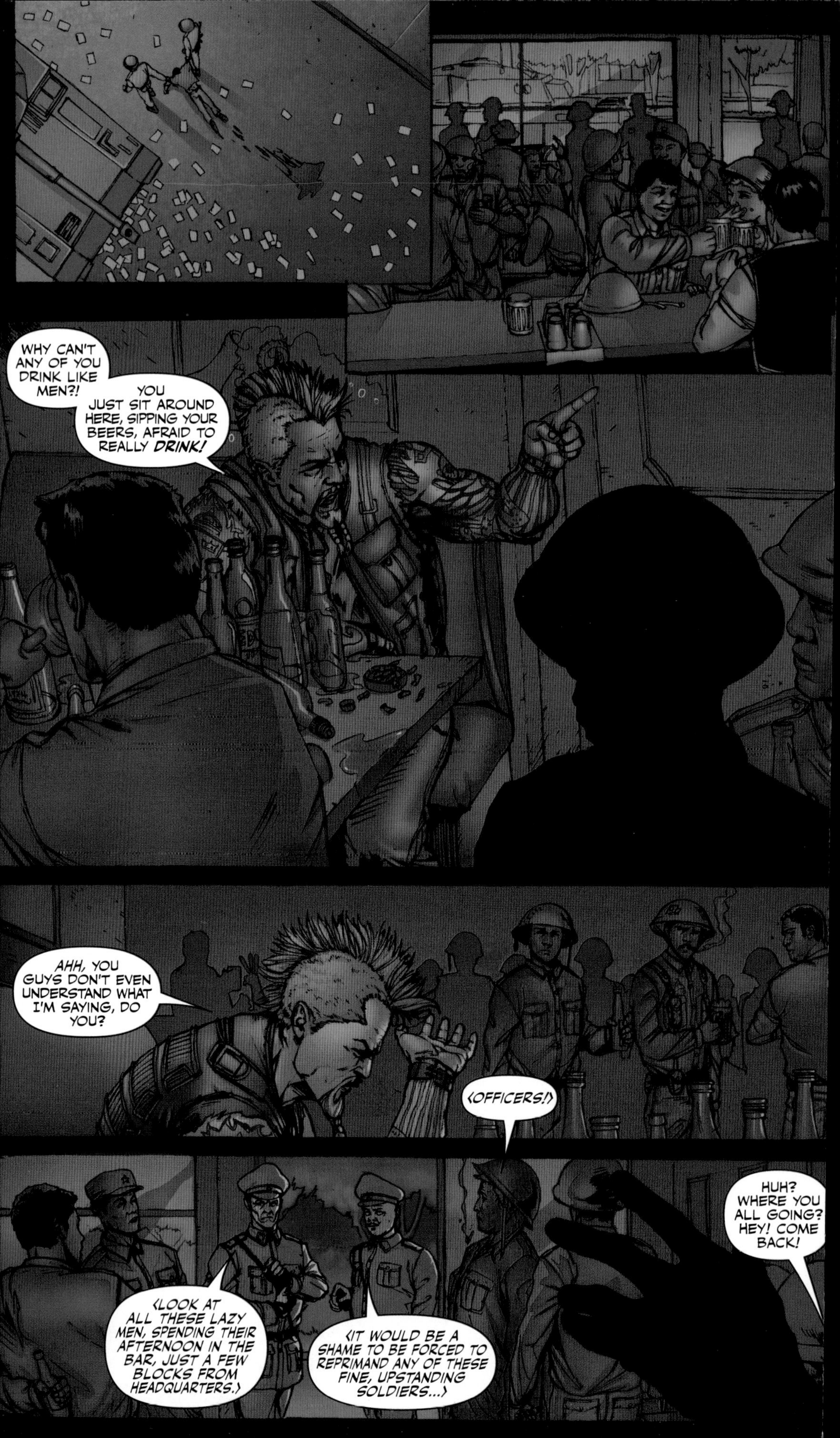
WHY CAN'T ANY OF YOU DRINK LIKE MEN?!
YOU JUST SIT AROUND HERE, SIPPING YOUR BEERS, AFRAID TO REALLY DRINK!
AHH, YOU GUYS DON'T EVEN UNDERSTAND WHAT I'M SAYING, DO YOU?
‹OFFICERS!›
‹LOOK AT ALL THESE LAZY MEN, SPENDING THEIR AFTERNOON IN THE BAR, JUST A FEW BLOCKS FROM HEADQUARTERS.›
‹IT WOULD BE A SHAME TO BE FORCED TO REPRIMAND ANY OF THESE FINE, UPSTANDING SOLDIERS...›
HUH? WHERE YOU ALL GOING? HEY! COME BACK!

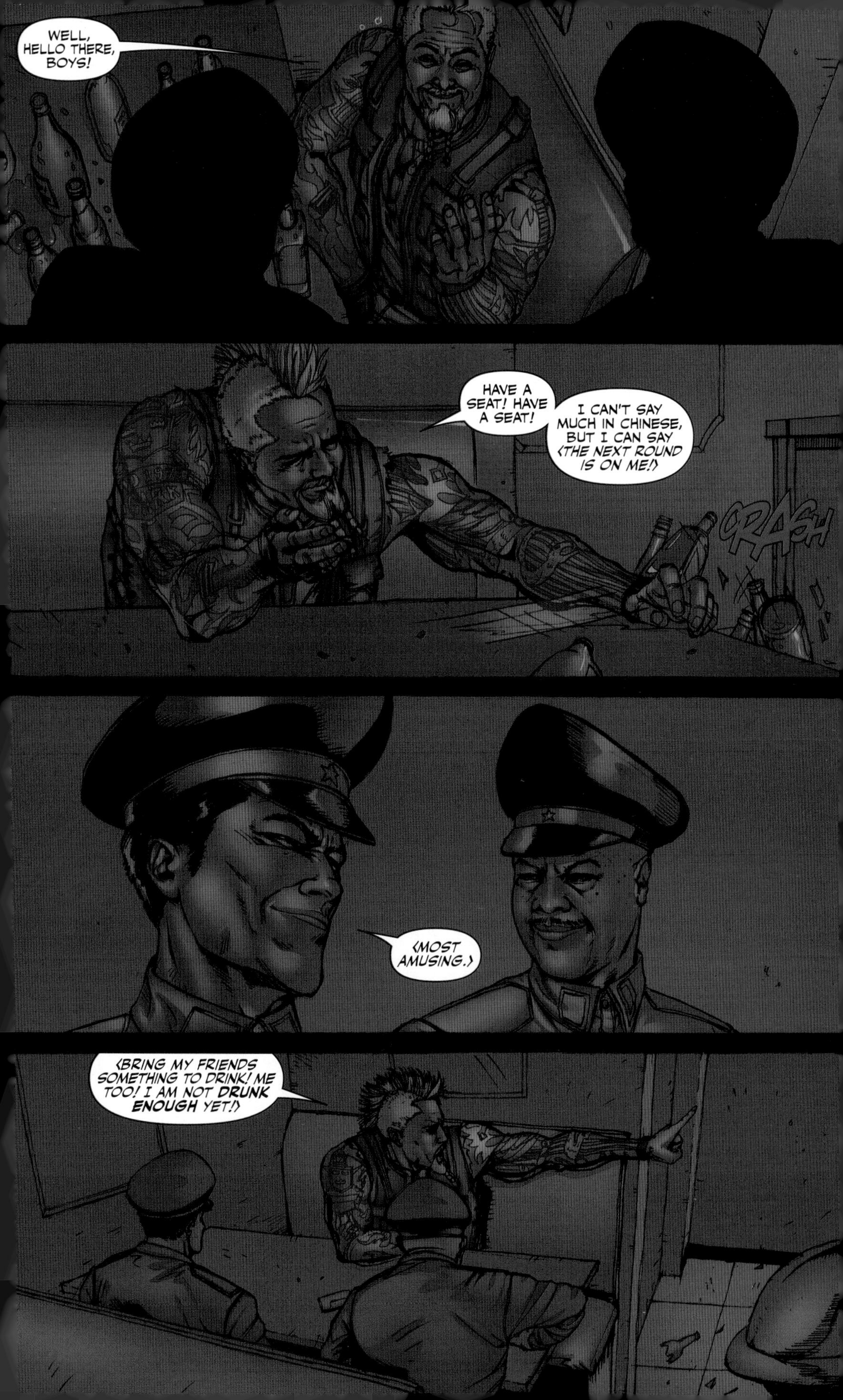
WELL, HELLO THERE, BOYS!
HAVE A SEAT! HAVE A SEAT!
I CAN'T SAY MUCH IN CHINESE, BUT I CAN SAY ‹THE NEXT ROUND IS ON ME!›
CRASH
‹MOST AMUSING.›
‹BRING MY FRIENDS SOMETHING TO DRINK! ME TOO! I AM NOT DRUNK ENOUGH YET!›

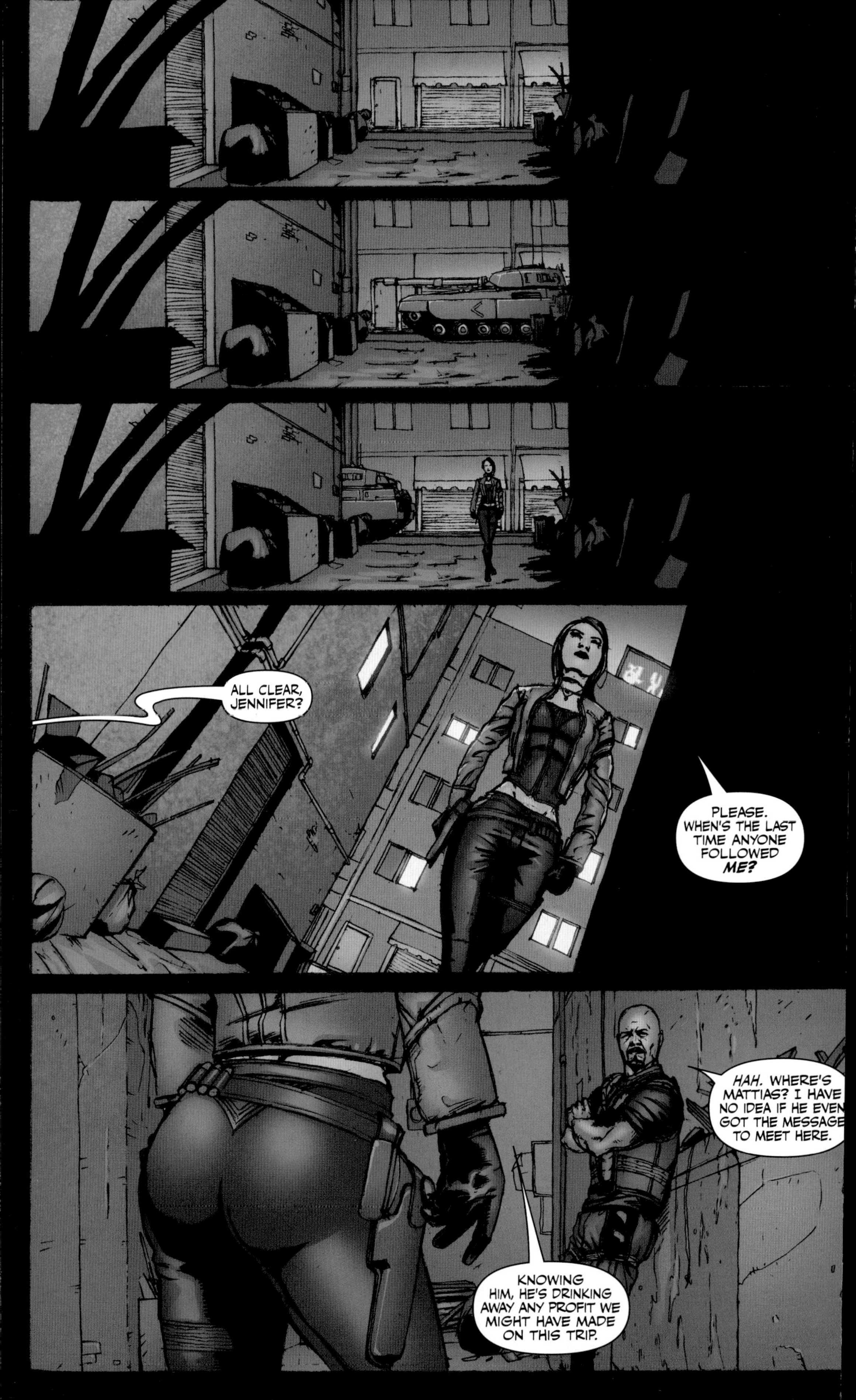
ALL CLEAR, JENNIFER?
PLEASE. WHEN'S THE LAST TIME ANYONE FOLLOWED *ME?*
HAH. WHERE'S MATTIAS? I HAVE NO IDEA IF HE EVEN GOT THE MESSAGE TO MEET HERE.
KNOWING HIM, HE'S DRINKING AWAY ANY PROFIT WE MIGHT HAVE MADE ON THIS TRIP.

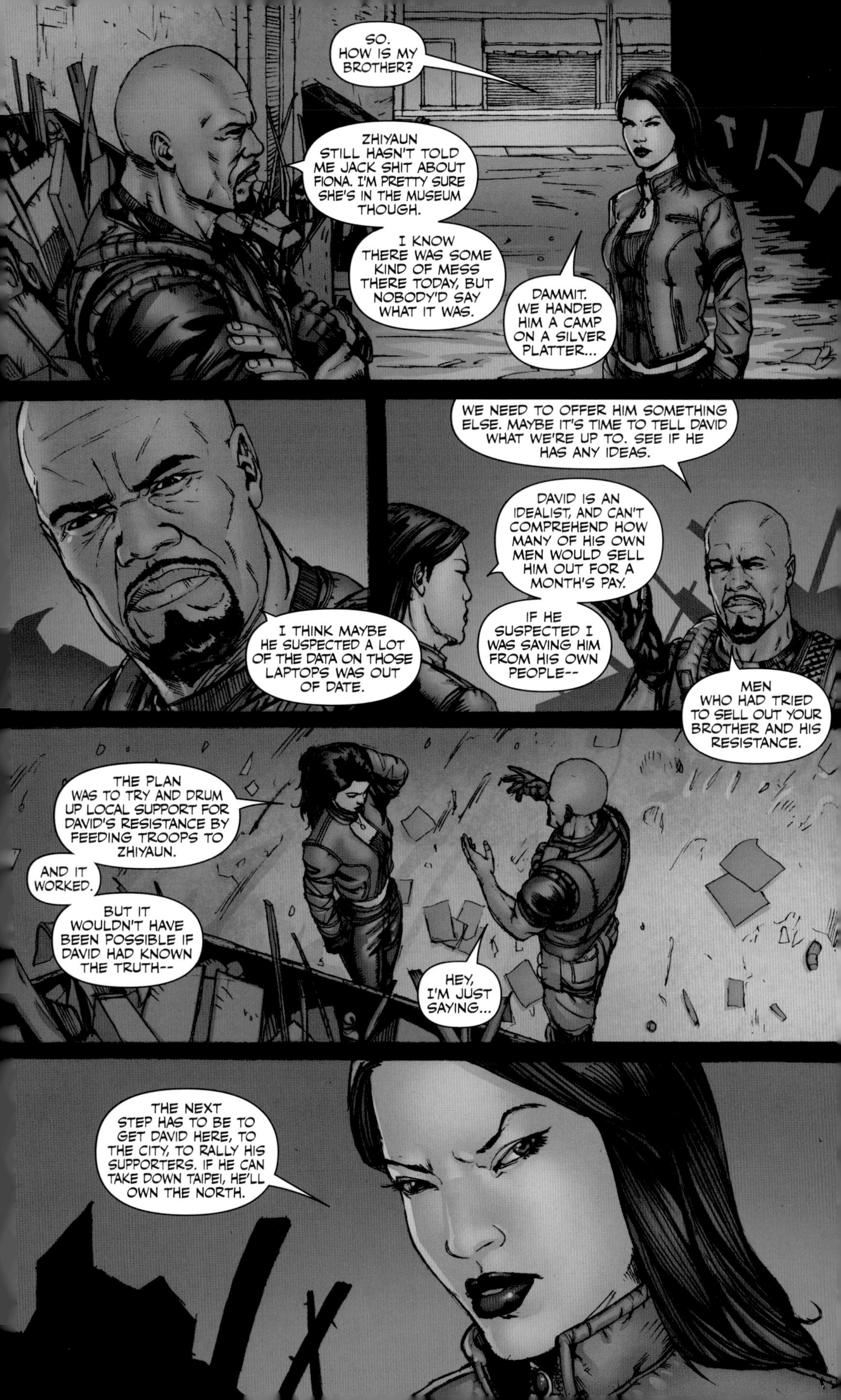
SO. HOW IS MY BROTHER?
ZHIYAUN STILL HASN'T TOLD ME JACK SHIT ABOUT FIONA. I'M PRETTY SURE SHE'S IN THE MUSEUM THOUGH.
I KNOW THERE WAS SOME KIND OF MESS THERE TODAY, BUT NOBODY'D SAY WHAT IT WAS.
DAMMIT. WE HANDED HIM A CAMP ON A SILVER PLATTER...
WE NEED TO OFFER HIM SOMETHING ELSE. MAYBE IT'S TIME TO TELL DAVID WHAT WE'RE UP TO. SEE IF HE HAS ANY IDEAS.
I THINK MAYBE HE SUSPECTED A LOT OF THE DATA ON THOSE LAPTOPS WAS OUT OF DATE.
DAVID IS AN IDEALIST, AND CAN'T COMPREHEND HOW MANY OF HIS OWN MEN WOULD SELL HIM OUT FOR A MONTH'S PAY.
IF HE SUSPECTED I WAS SAVING HIM FROM HIS OWN PEOPLE--
MEN WHO HAD TRIED TO SELL OUT YOUR BROTHER AND HIS RESISTANCE.
THE PLAN WAS TO TRY AND DRUM UP LOCAL SUPPORT FOR DAVID'S RESISTANCE BY FEEDING TROOPS TO ZHIYAUN.
AND IT WORKED.
BUT IT WOULDN'T HAVE BEEN POSSIBLE IF DAVID HAD KNOWN THE TRUTH--
HEY, I'M JUST SAYING...
THE NEXT STEP HAS TO BE TO GET DAVID HERE, TO THE CITY, TO RALLY HIS SUPPORTERS. IF HE CAN TAKE DOWN TAIPEI, HE'LL OWN THE NORTH.

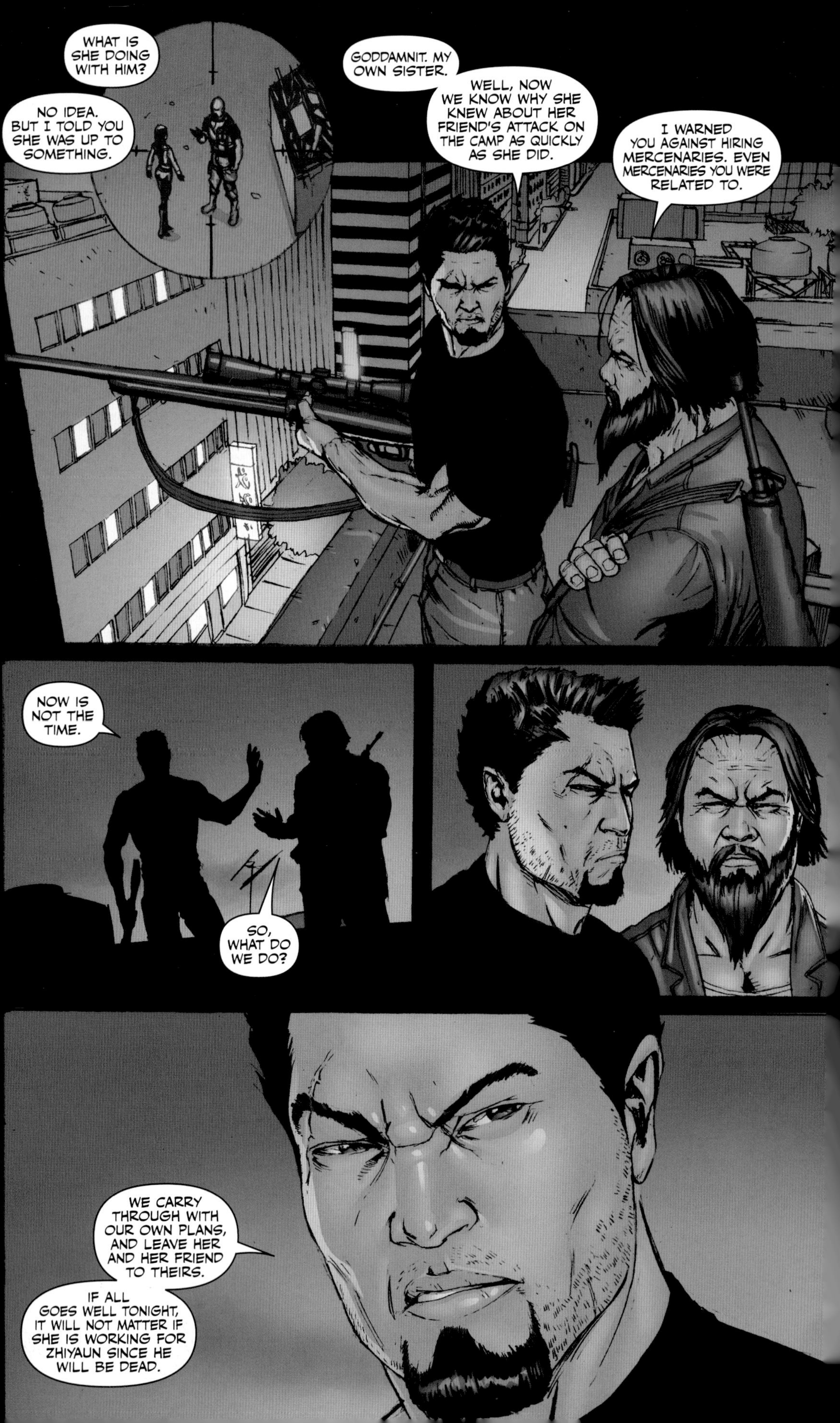
WHAT IS SHE DOING WITH HIM?
NO IDEA. BUT I TOLD YOU SHE WAS UP TO SOMETHING.
GODDAMNIT. MY OWN SISTER.
WELL, NOW WE KNOW WHY SHE KNEW ABOUT HER FRIEND'S ATTACK ON THE CAMP AS QUICKLY AS SHE DID.
I WARNED YOU AGAINST HIRING MERCENARIES. EVEN MERCENARIES YOU WERE RELATED TO.
NOW IS NOT THE TIME.
SO, WHAT DO WE DO?
WE CARRY THROUGH WITH OUR OWN PLANS, AND LEAVE HER AND HER FRIEND TO THEIRS.
IF ALL GOES WELL TONIGHT, IT WILL NOT MATTER IF SHE IS WORKING FOR ZHIYAUN SINCE HE WILL BE DEAD.

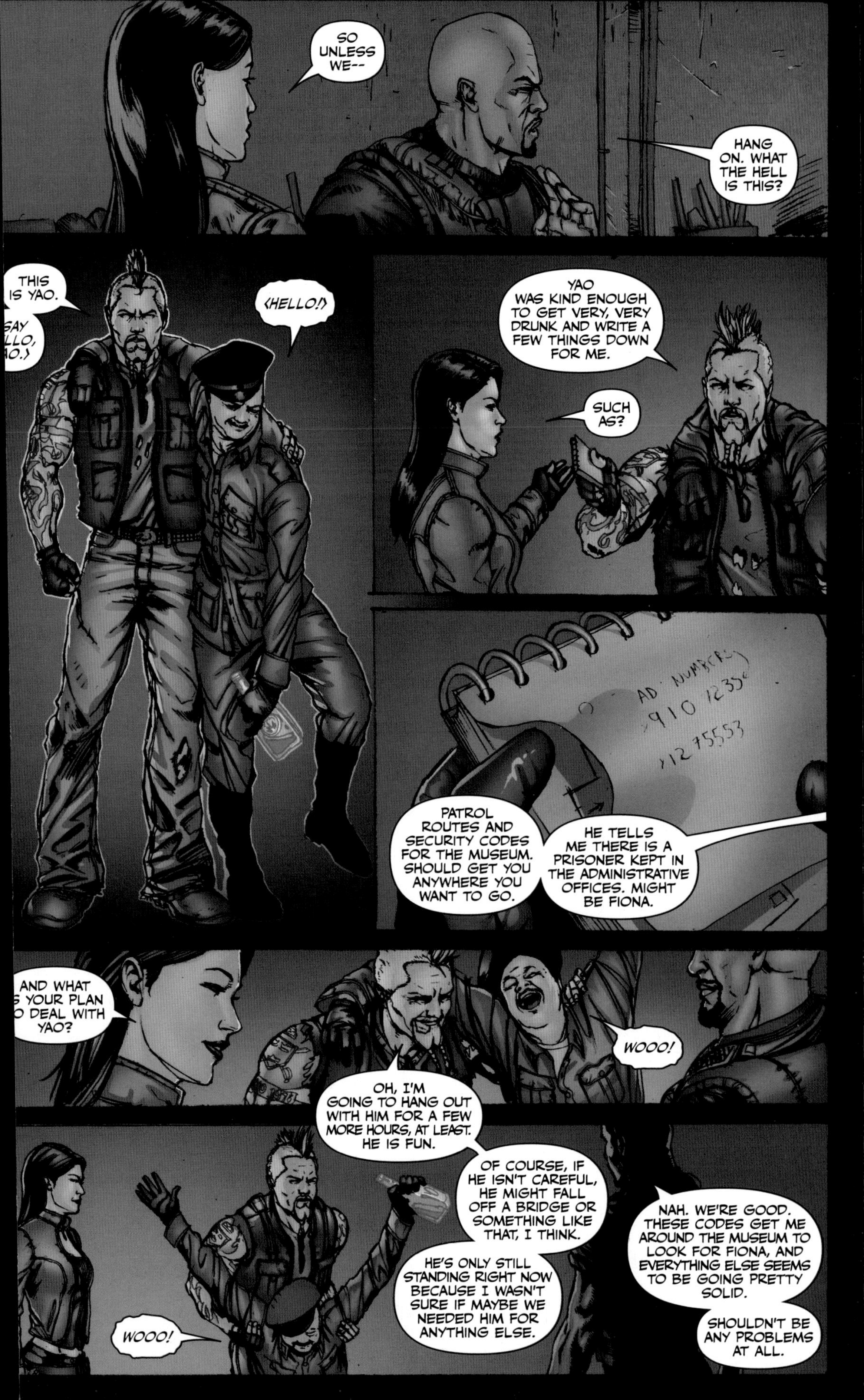
SO UNLESS WE--
HANG ON. WHAT THE HELL IS THIS?
THIS IS YAO.
SAY LLO, AO.>
<HELLO!>
YAO WAS KIND ENOUGH TO GET VERY, VERY DRUNK AND WRITE A FEW THINGS DOWN FOR ME.
SUCH AS?
AD NUMBERS
PATROL ROUTES AND SECURITY CODES FOR THE MUSEUM. SHOULD GET YOU ANYWHERE YOU WANT TO GO.
HE TELLS ME THERE IS A PRISONER KEPT IN THE ADMINISTRATIVE OFFICES. MIGHT BE FIONA.
AND WHAT S YOUR PLAN O DEAL WITH YAO?
WOOO!
OH, I'M GOING TO HANG OUT WITH HIM FOR A FEW MORE HOURS, AT LEAST. HE IS FUN.
OF COURSE, IF HE ISN'T CAREFUL, HE MIGHT FALL OFF A BRIDGE OR SOMETHING LIKE THAT, I THINK.
HE'S ONLY STILL STANDING RIGHT NOW BECAUSE I WASN'T SURE IF MAYBE WE NEEDED HIM FOR ANYTHING ELSE.
WOOO!
NAH. WE'RE GOOD. THESE CODES GET ME AROUND THE MUSEUM TO LOOK FOR FIONA, AND EVERYTHING ELSE SEEMS TO BE GOING PRETTY SOLID.
SHOULDN'T BE ANY PROBLEMS AT ALL.

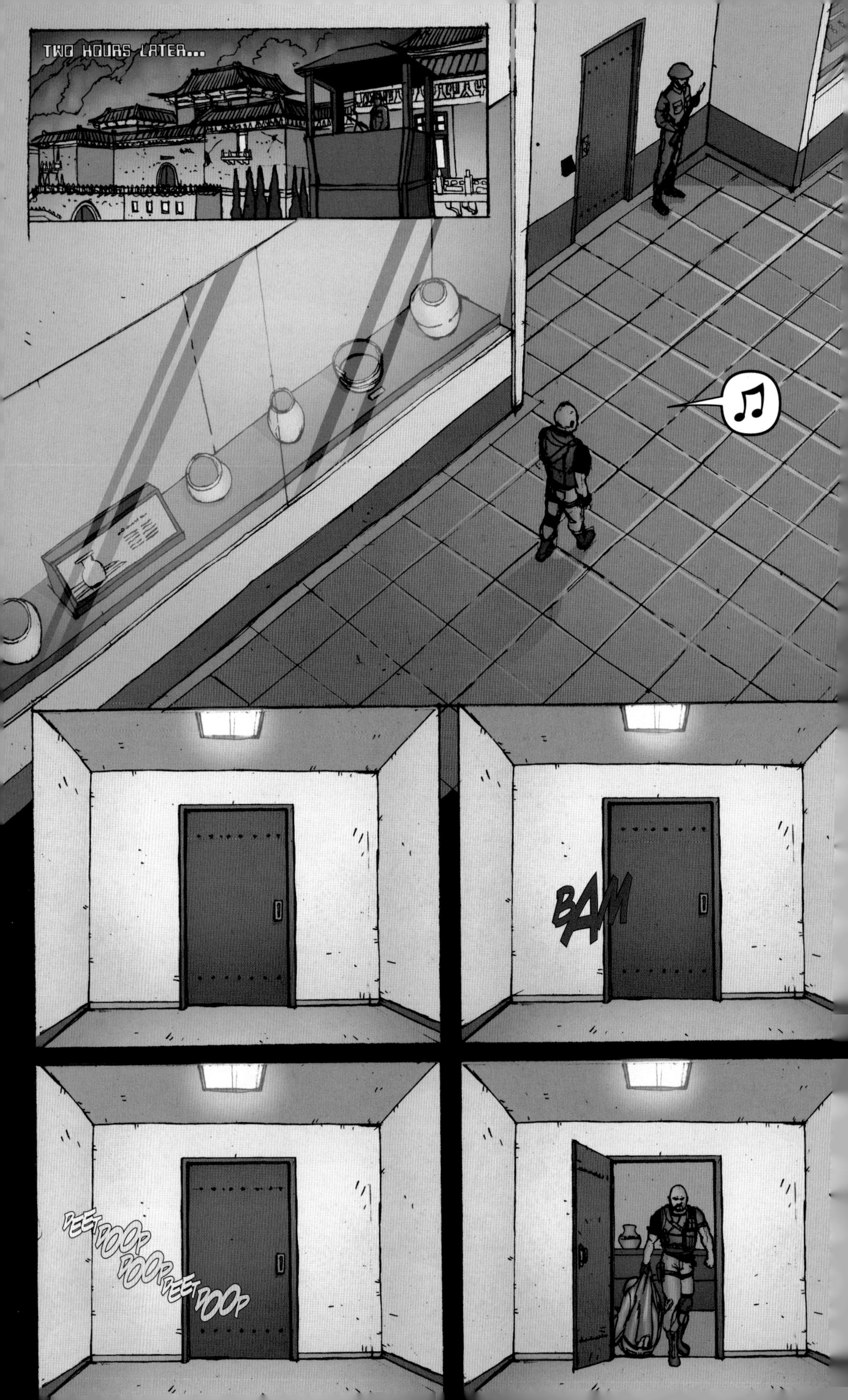
TWO HOURS LATER...
♫
BAM
DEETDOOP DOOPDEETDOOP

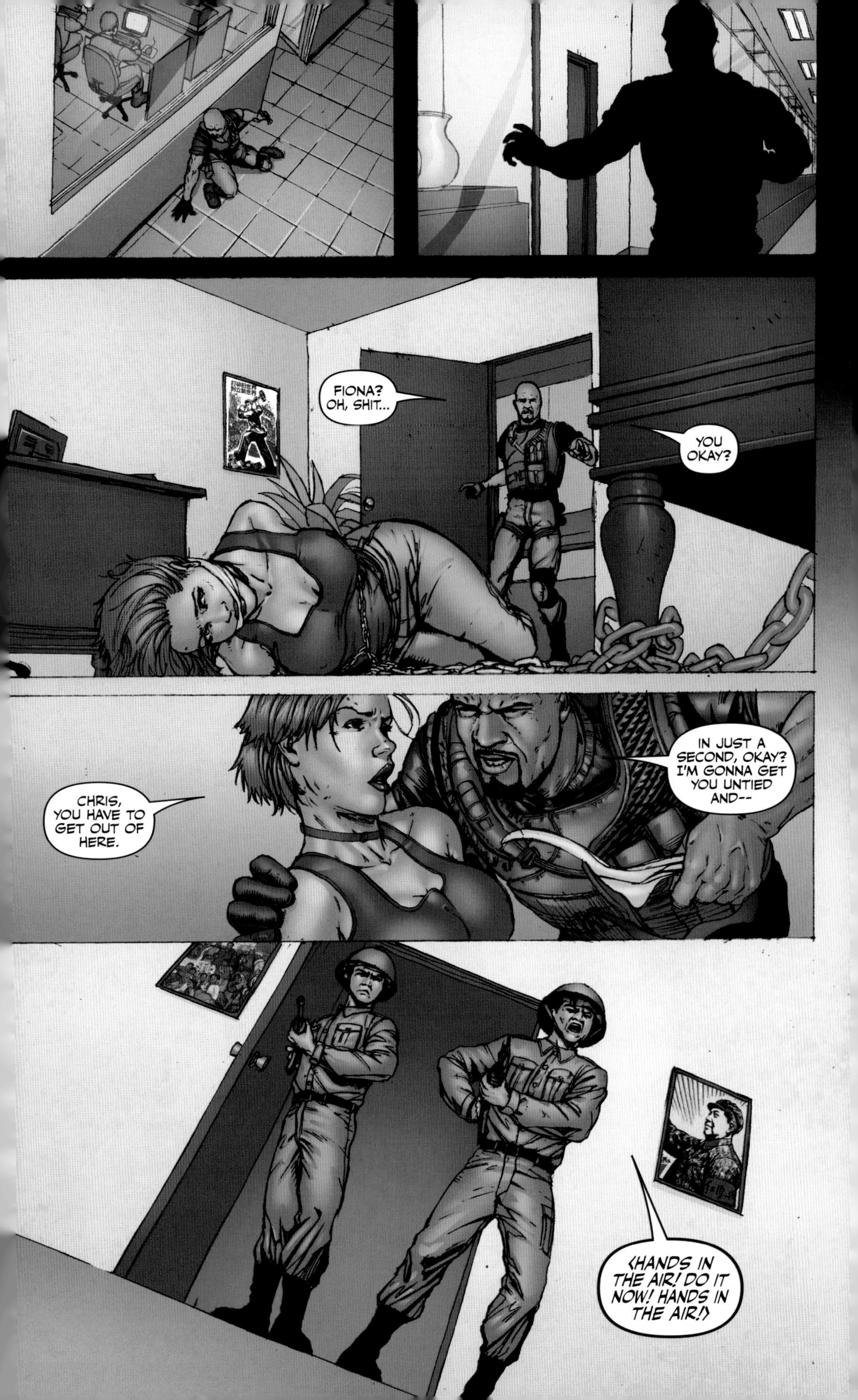
FIONA? OH, SHIT...
YOU OKAY?
IN JUST A SECOND, OKAY? I'M GONNA GET YOU UNTIED AND--
CHRIS, YOU HAVE TO GET OUT OF HERE.
‹HANDS IN THE AIR! DO IT NOW! HANDS IN THE AIR!›

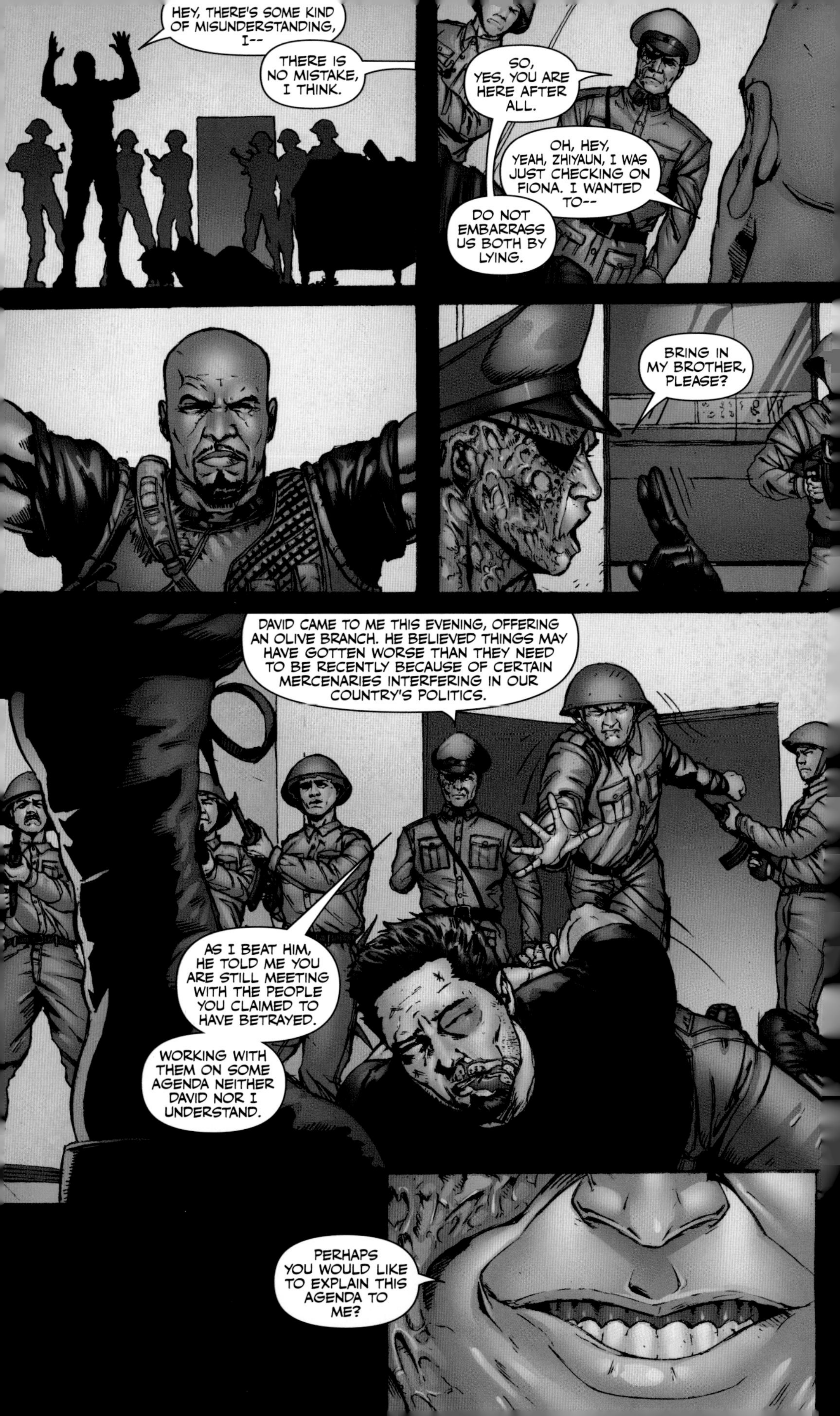
HEY, THERE'S SOME KIND OF MISUNDERSTANDING, I--
THERE IS NO MISTAKE, I THINK.
SO, YES, YOU ARE HERE AFTER ALL.
OH, HEY, YEAH, ZHIYAUN, I WAS JUST CHECKING ON FIONA. I WANTED TO--
DO NOT EMBARRASS US BOTH BY LYING.
BRING IN MY BROTHER, PLEASE?
DAVID CAME TO ME THIS EVENING, OFFERING AN OLIVE BRANCH. HE BELIEVED THINGS MAY HAVE GOTTEN WORSE THAN THEY NEED TO BE RECENTLY BECAUSE OF CERTAIN MERCENARIES INTERFERING IN OUR COUNTRY'S POLITICS.
AS I BEAT HIM, HE TOLD ME YOU ARE STILL MEETING WITH THE PEOPLE YOU CLAIMED TO HAVE BETRAYED.
WORKING WITH THEM ON SOME AGENDA NEITHER DAVID NOR I UNDERSTAND.
PERHAPS YOU WOULD LIKE TO EXPLAIN THIS AGENDA TO ME?

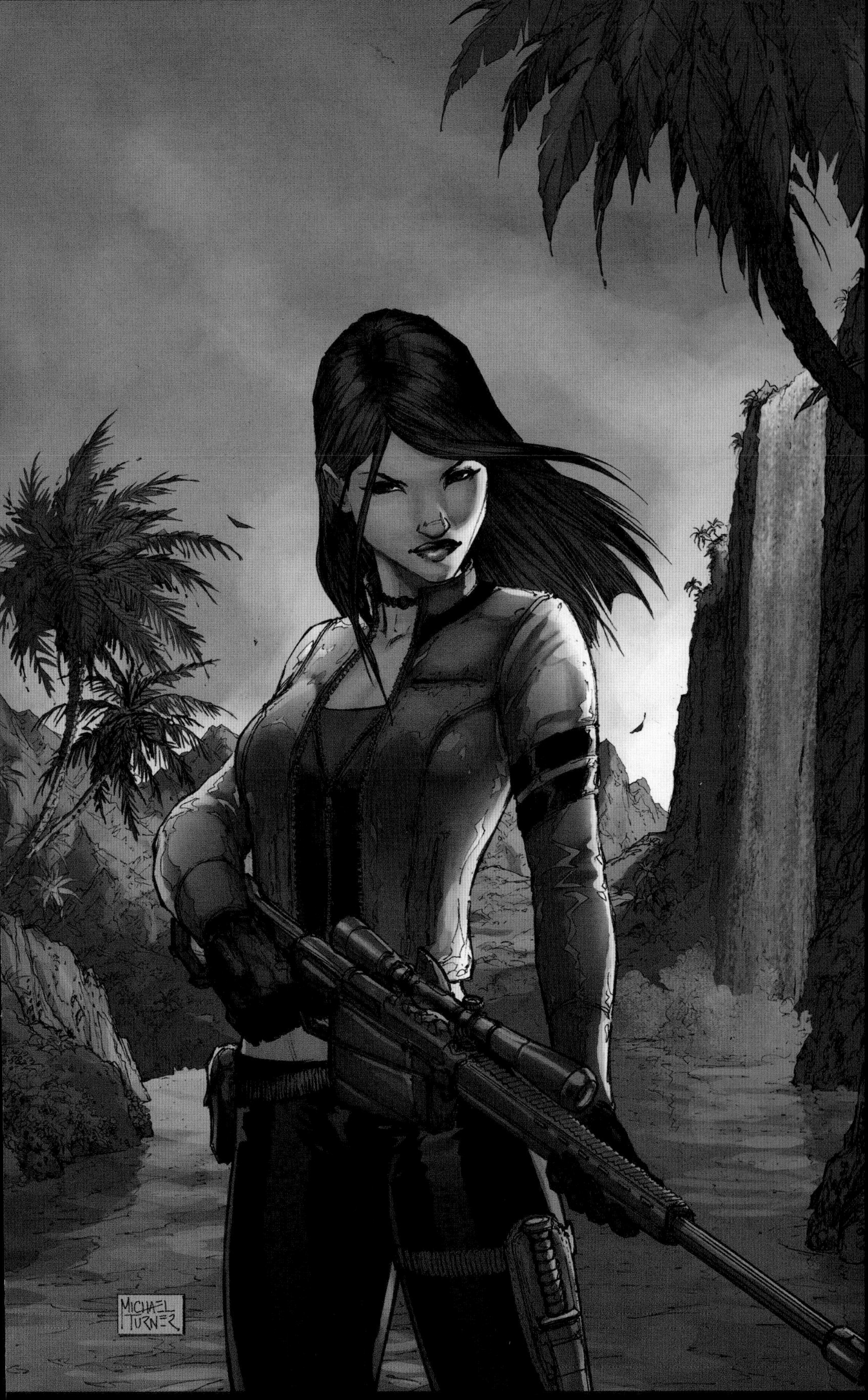
MICHAEL TURNER

CHAPTER THREE

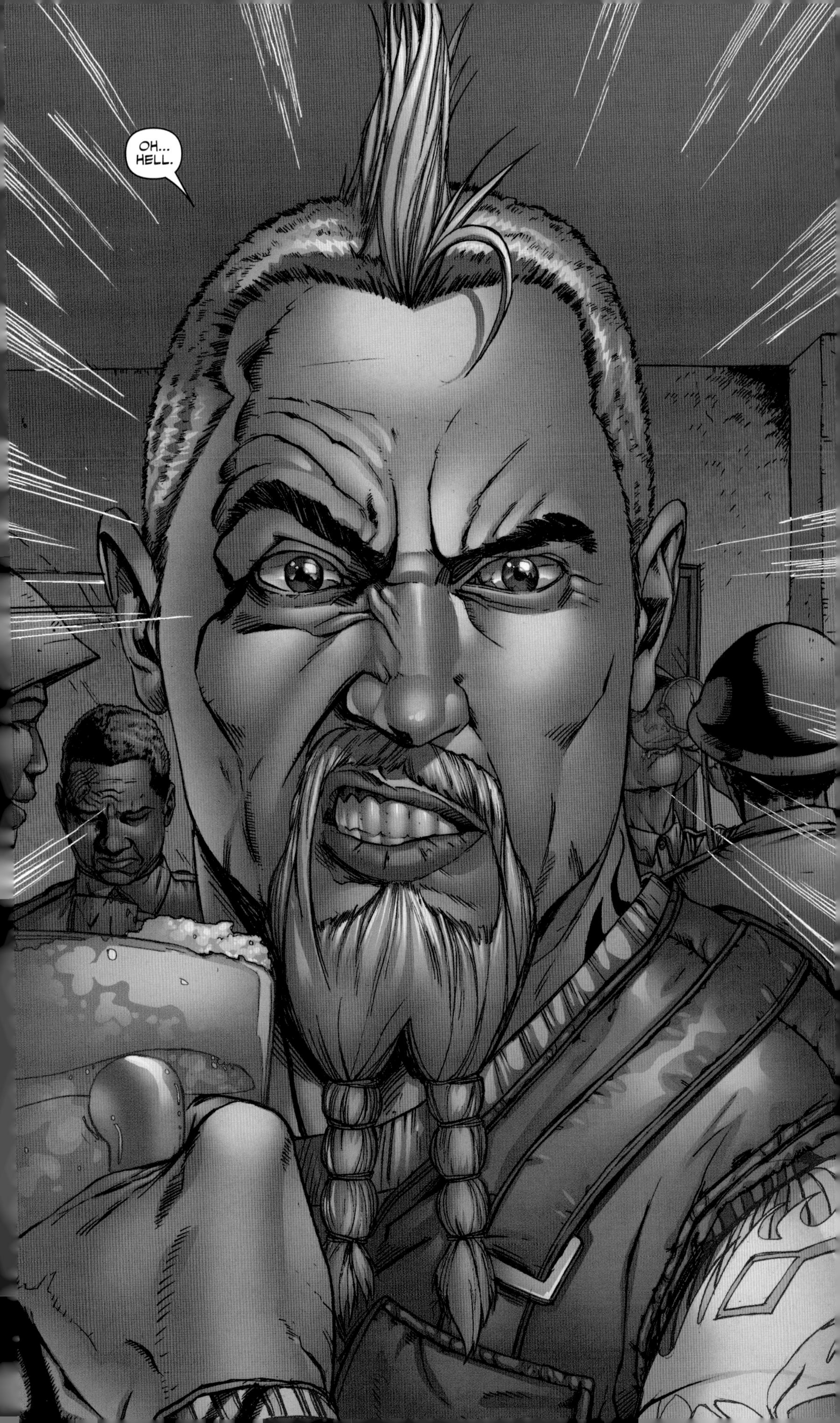
OH... HELL.

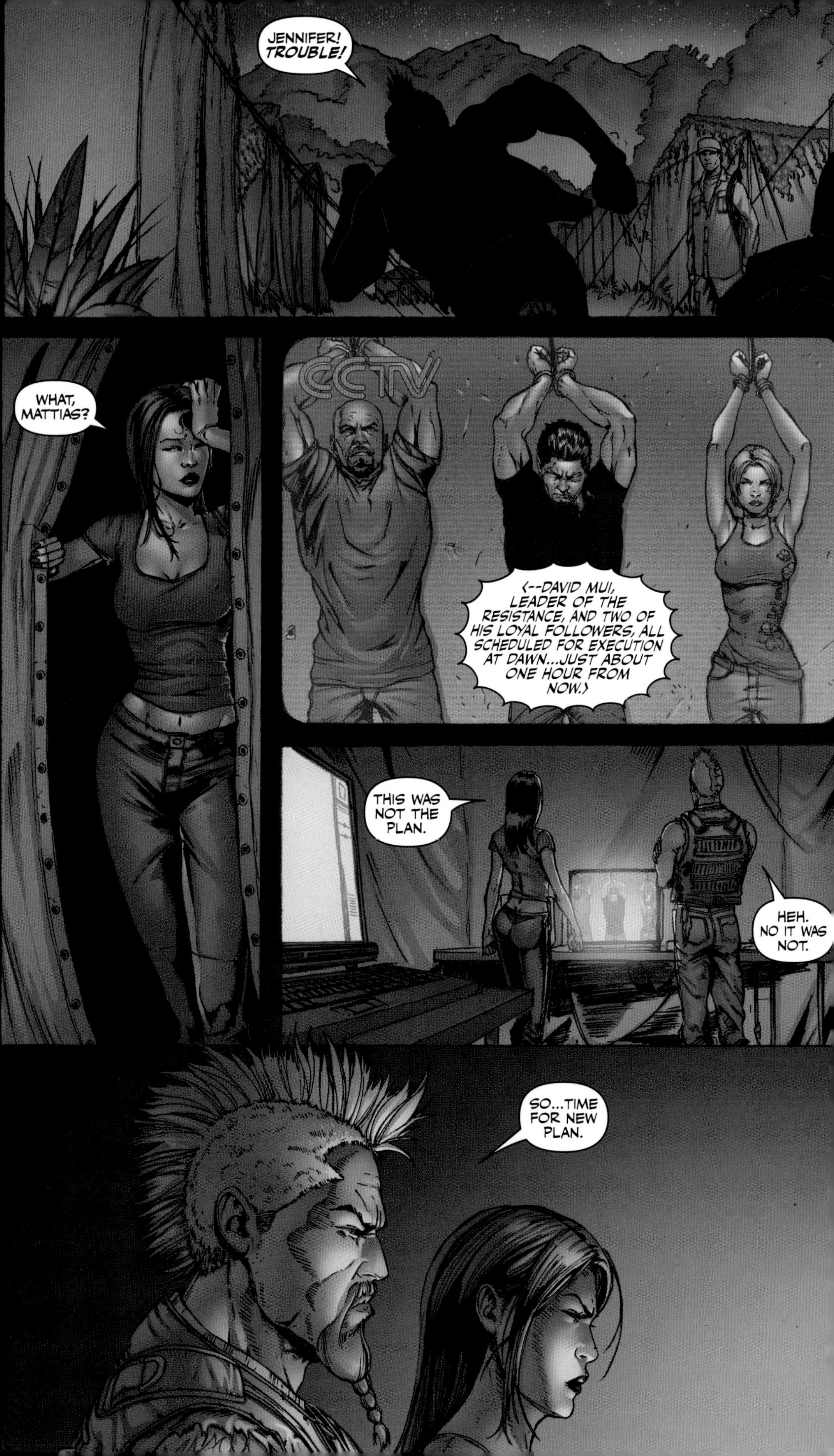
JENNIFER! TROUBLE!
WHAT, MATTIAS?
CCTV
<--DAVID MUI, LEADER OF THE RESISTANCE, AND TWO OF HIS LOYAL FOLLOWERS, ALL SCHEDULED FOR EXECUTION AT DAWN...JUST ABOUT ONE HOUR FROM NOW.>
THIS WAS NOT THE PLAN.
HEH. NO IT WAS NOT.
SO...TIME FOR NEW PLAN.

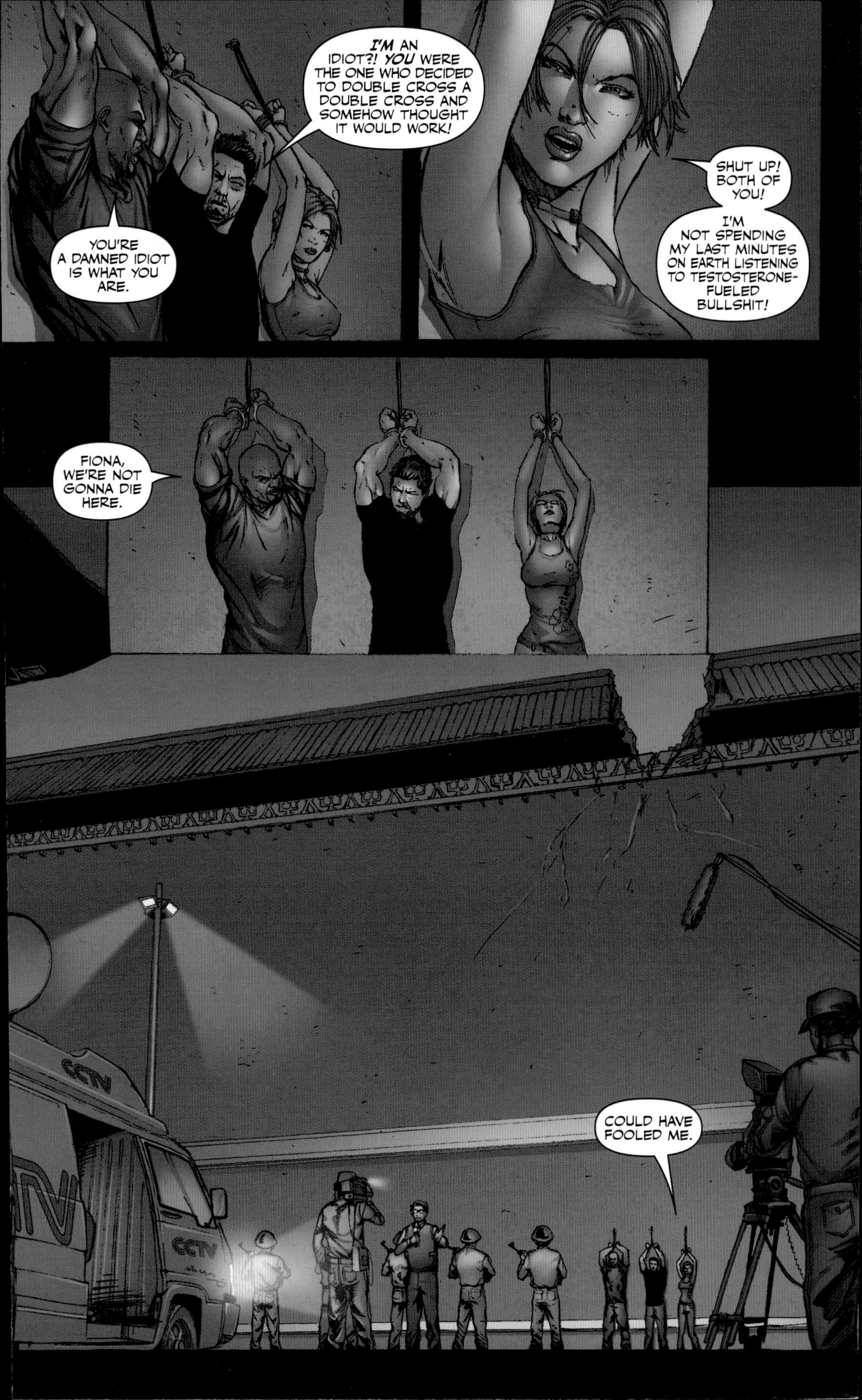
I'M AN IDIOT?! YOU WERE THE ONE WHO DECIDED TO DOUBLE CROSS A DOUBLE CROSS AND SOMEHOW THOUGHT IT WOULD WORK!
YOU'RE A DAMNED IDIOT IS WHAT YOU ARE.
SHUT UP! BOTH OF YOU!
I'M NOT SPENDING MY LAST MINUTES ON EARTH LISTENING TO TESTOSTERONE-FUELED BULLSHIT!
FIONA, WE'RE NOT GONNA DIE HERE.
CCTV
COULD HAVE FOOLED ME.

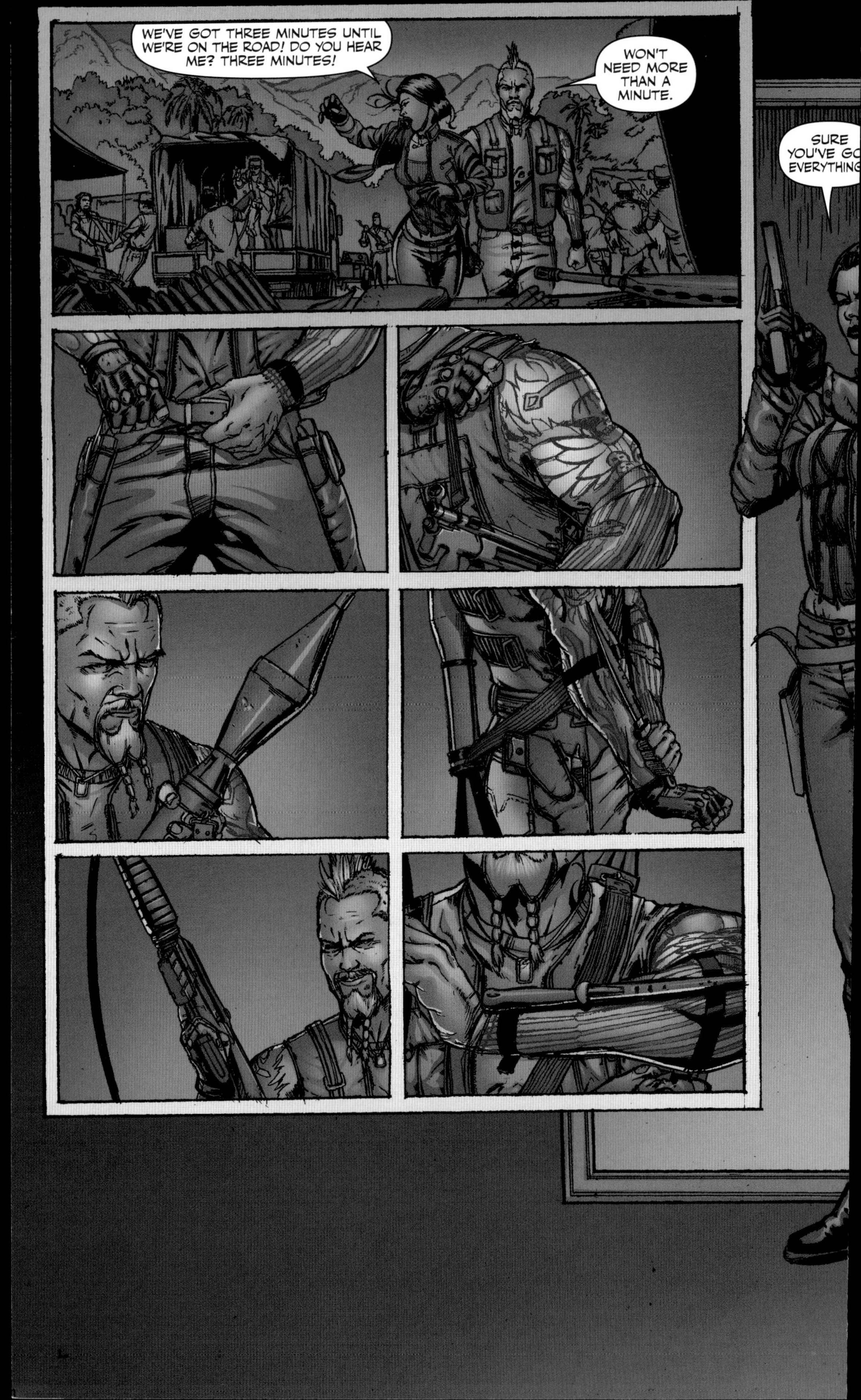

WE'VE GOT THREE MINUTES UNTIL WE'RE ON THE ROAD! DO YOU HEAR ME? THREE MINUTES!
WON'T NEED MORE THAN A MINUTE.
SURE
YOU'VE GO
EVERYTHING

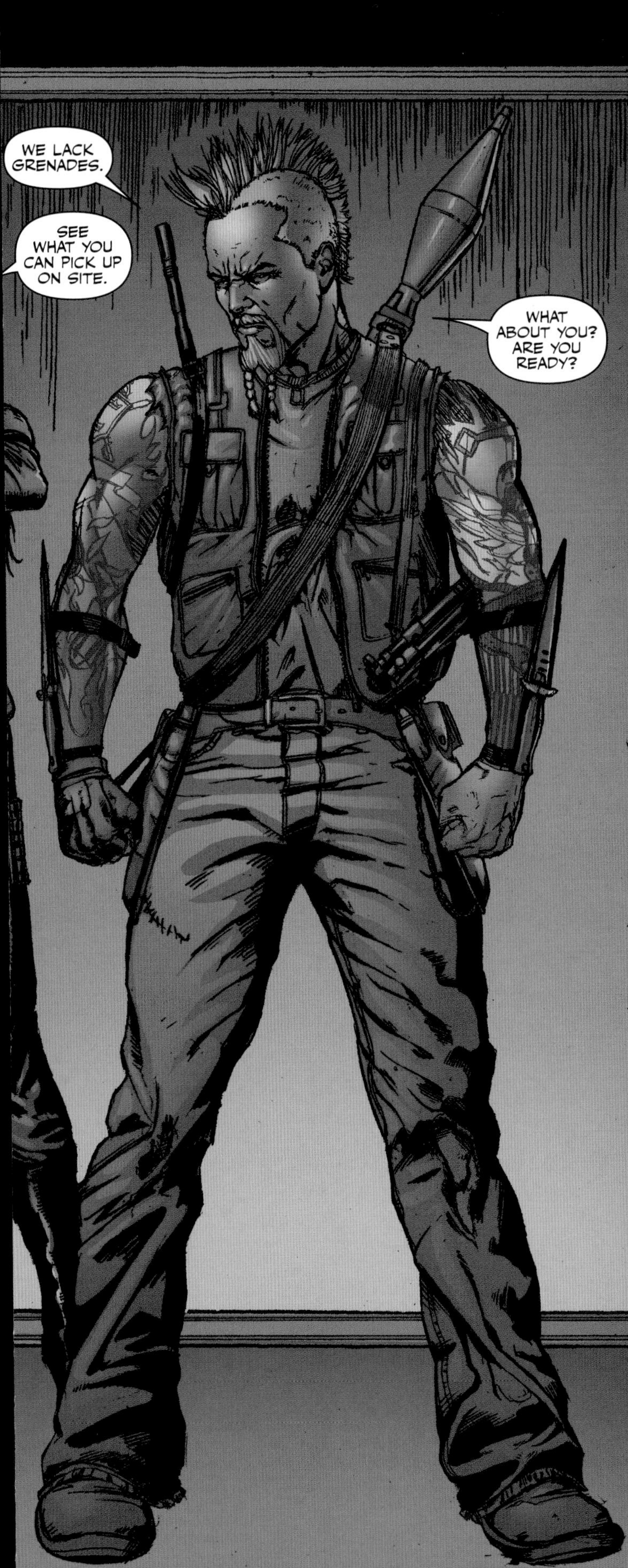
WE LACK GRENADES.
SEE WHAT YOU CAN PICK UP ON SITE.
WHAT ABOUT YOU? ARE YOU READY?
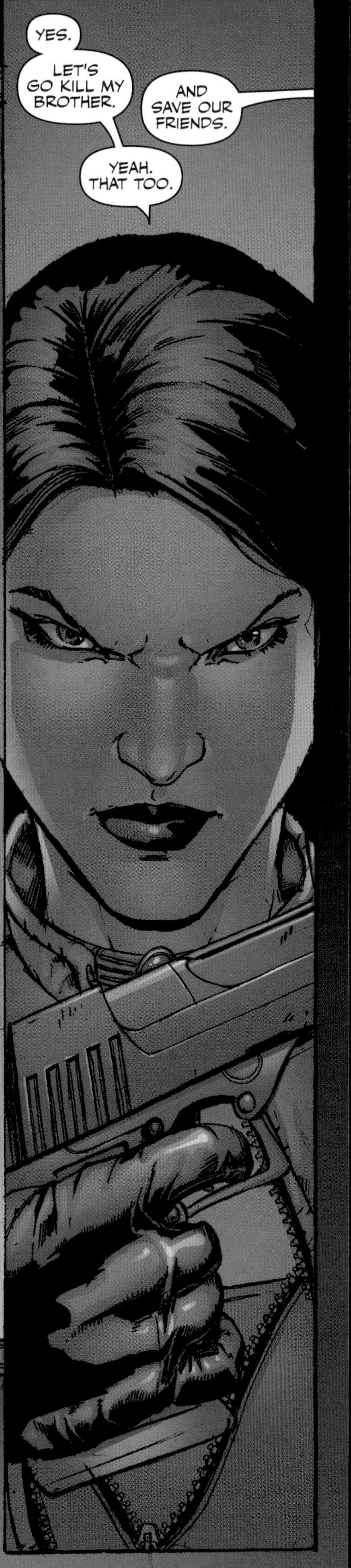
YES.
LET'S GO KILL MY BROTHER.
AND SAVE OUR FRIENDS.
YEAH. THAT TOO.

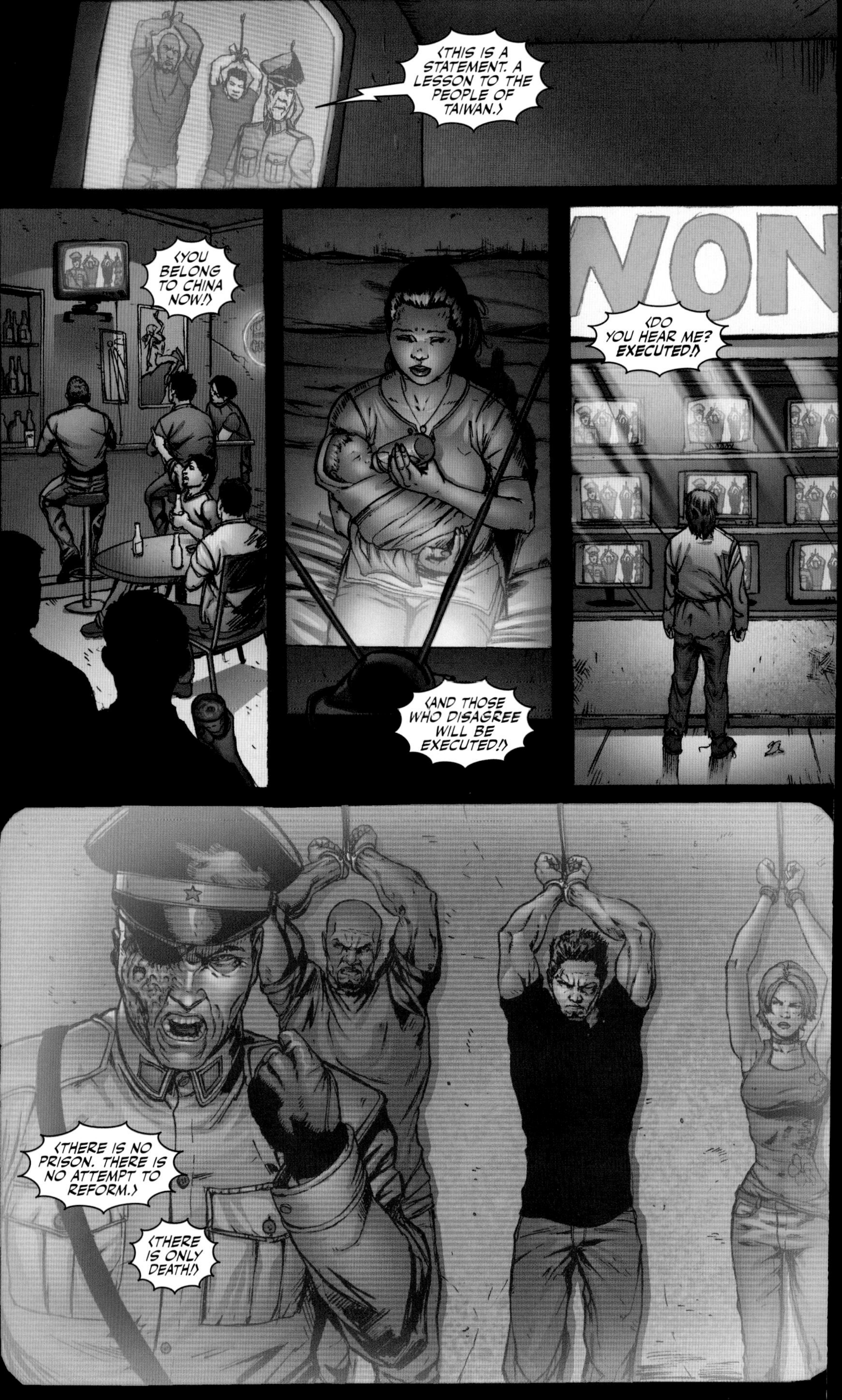
‹THIS IS A STATEMENT. A LESSON TO THE PEOPLE OF TAIWAN.›
‹YOU BELONG TO CHINA NOW!›
‹AND THOSE WHO DISAGREE WILL BE EXECUTED!›
NON
‹DO YOU HEAR ME? EXECUTED!›
‹THERE IS NO PRISON. THERE IS NO ATTEMPT TO REFORM.›
‹THERE IS ONLY DEATH!›

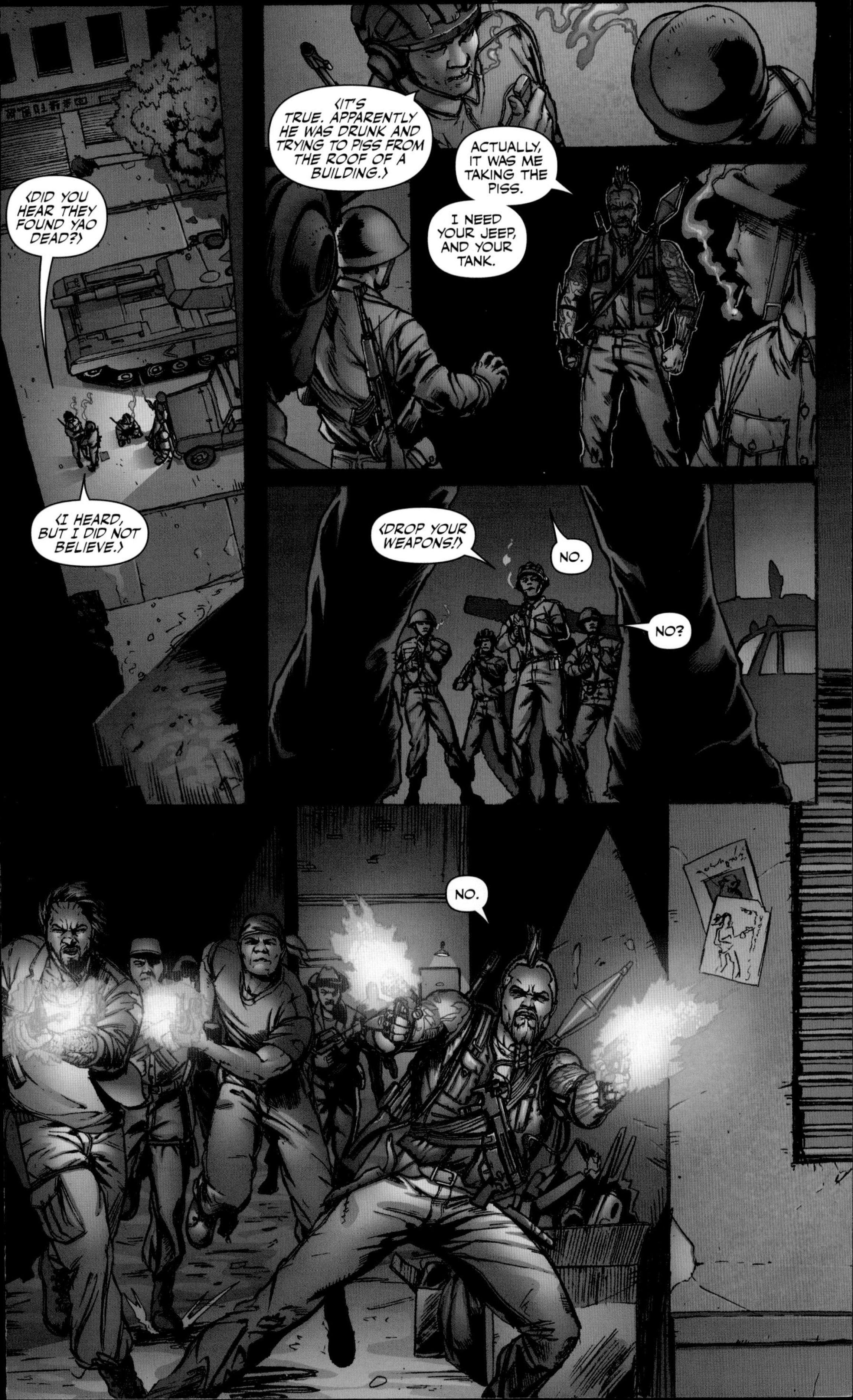
‹DID YOU HEAR THEY FOUND YAO DEAD?›
‹IT'S TRUE. APPARENTLY HE WAS DRUNK AND TRYING TO PISS FROM THE ROOF OF A BUILDING.›
‹I HEARD, BUT I DID NOT BELIEVE.›
ACTUALLY, IT WAS ME TAKING THE PISS.
I NEED YOUR JEEP, AND YOUR TANK.
‹DROP YOUR WEAPONS!›
NO.
NO?
NO.

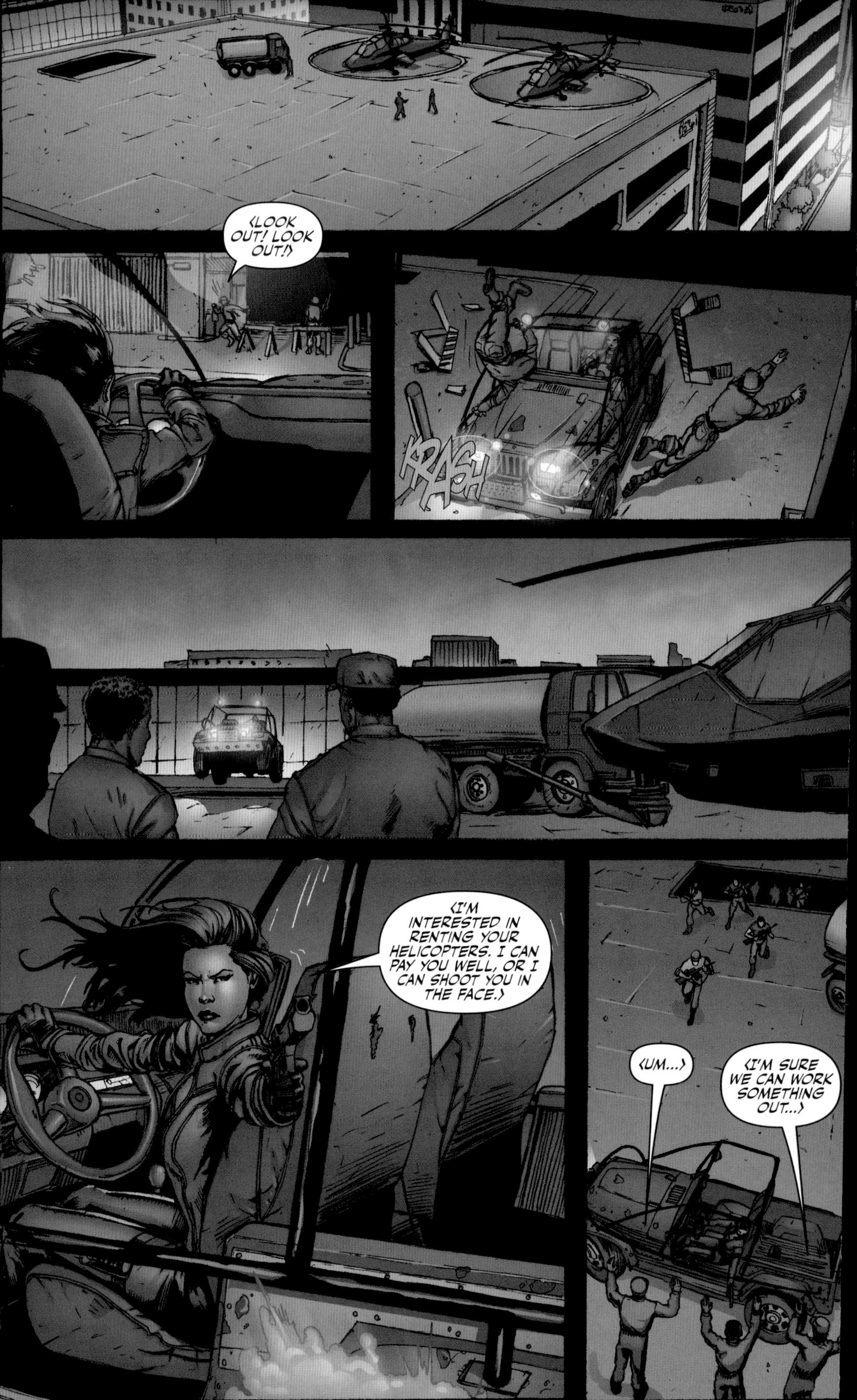
‹LOOK OUT! LOOK OUT!›
KRASH
‹I'M INTERESTED IN RENTING YOUR HELICOPTERS. I CAN PAY YOU WELL, OR I CAN SHOOT YOU IN THE FACE.›
‹UM...›
‹I'M SURE WE CAN WORK SOMETHING OUT...›

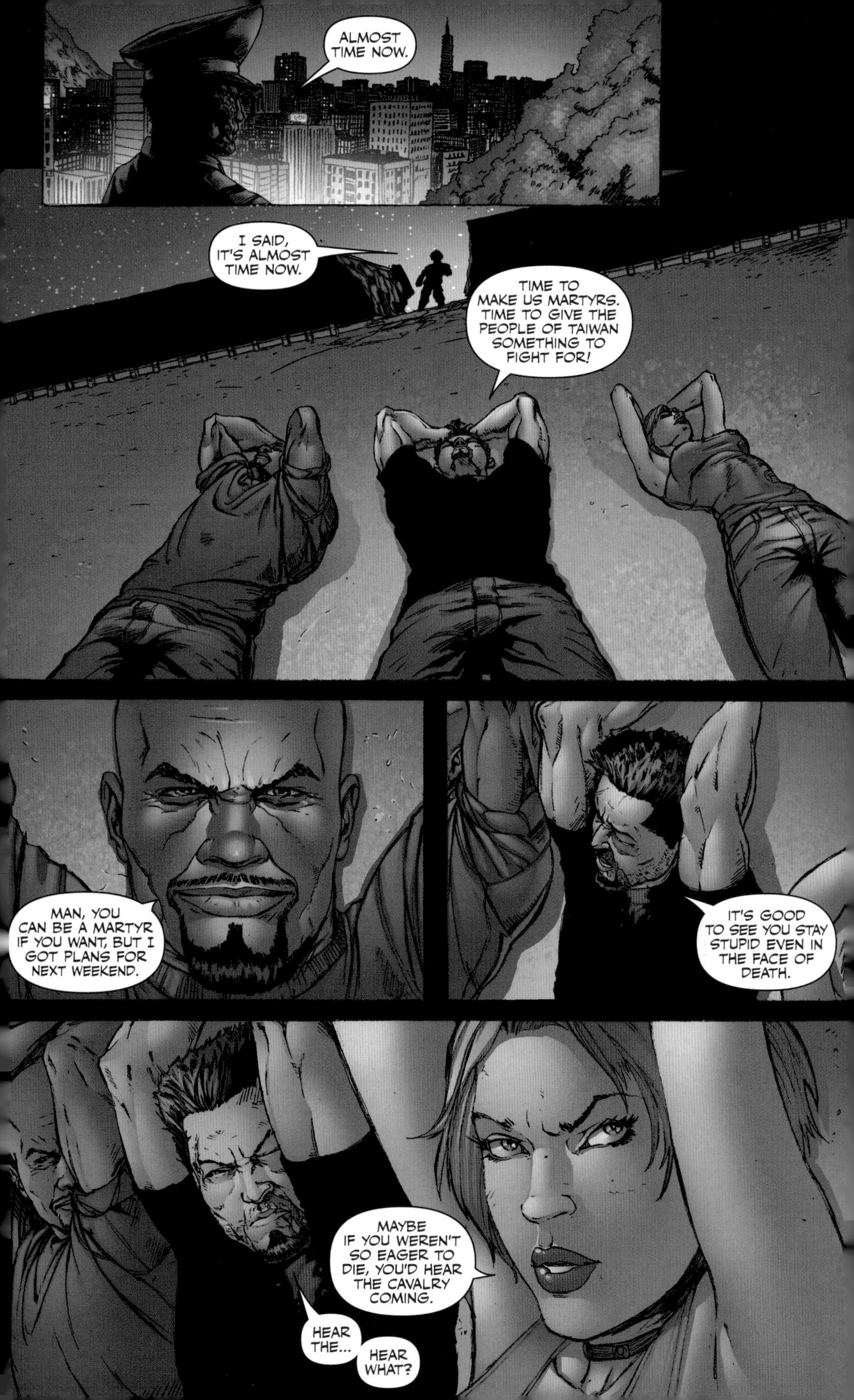
ALMOST TIME NOW.
I SAID, IT'S ALMOST TIME NOW.
TIME TO MAKE US MARTYRS. TIME TO GIVE THE PEOPLE OF TAIWAN SOMETHING TO FIGHT FOR!
MAN, YOU CAN BE A MARTYR IF YOU WANT, BUT I GOT PLANS FOR NEXT WEEKEND.
IT'S GOOD TO SEE YOU STAY STUPID EVEN IN THE FACE OF DEATH.
MAYBE IF YOU WEREN'T SO EAGER TO DIE, YOU'D HEAR THE CAVALRY COMING.
HEAR THE...
HEAR WHAT?

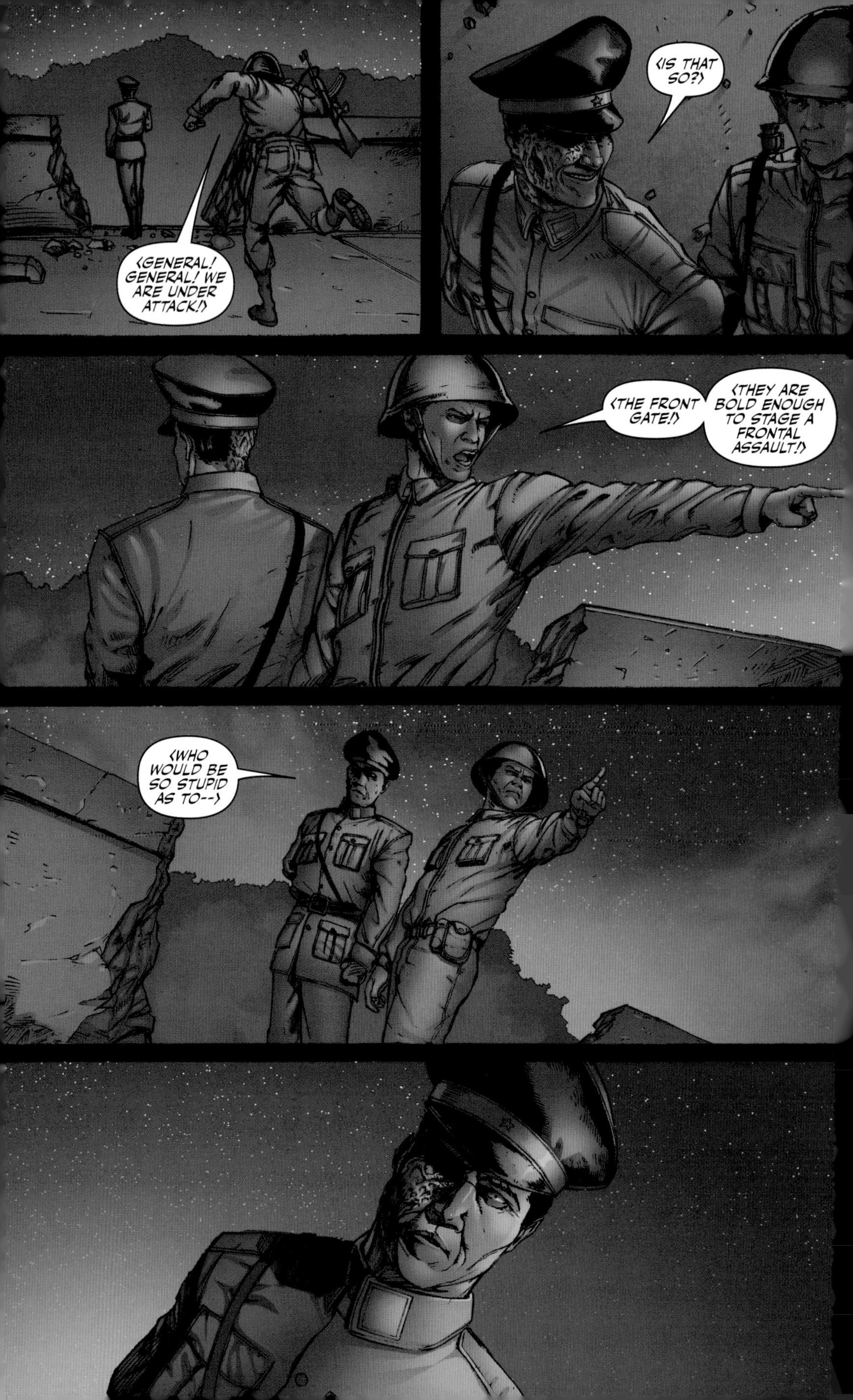
‹GENERAL! GENERAL! WE ARE UNDER ATTACK!›
‹IS THAT SO?›
‹THE FRONT GATE!›
‹THEY ARE BOLD ENOUGH TO STAGE A FRONTAL ASSAULT!›
‹WHO WOULD BE SO STUPID AS TO--›

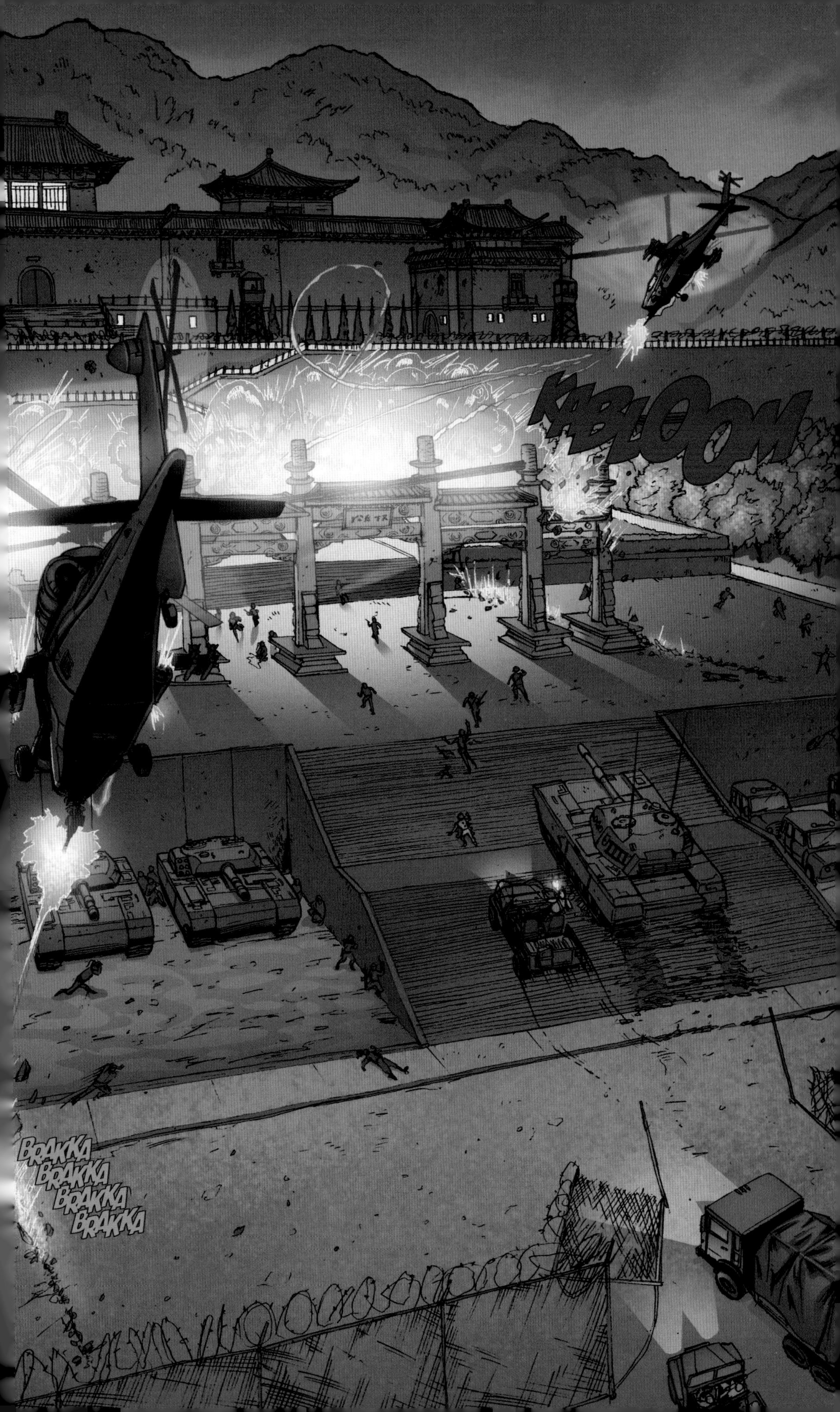
KABLOOM
BRAKKA
BRAKKA
BRAKKA
BRAKKA

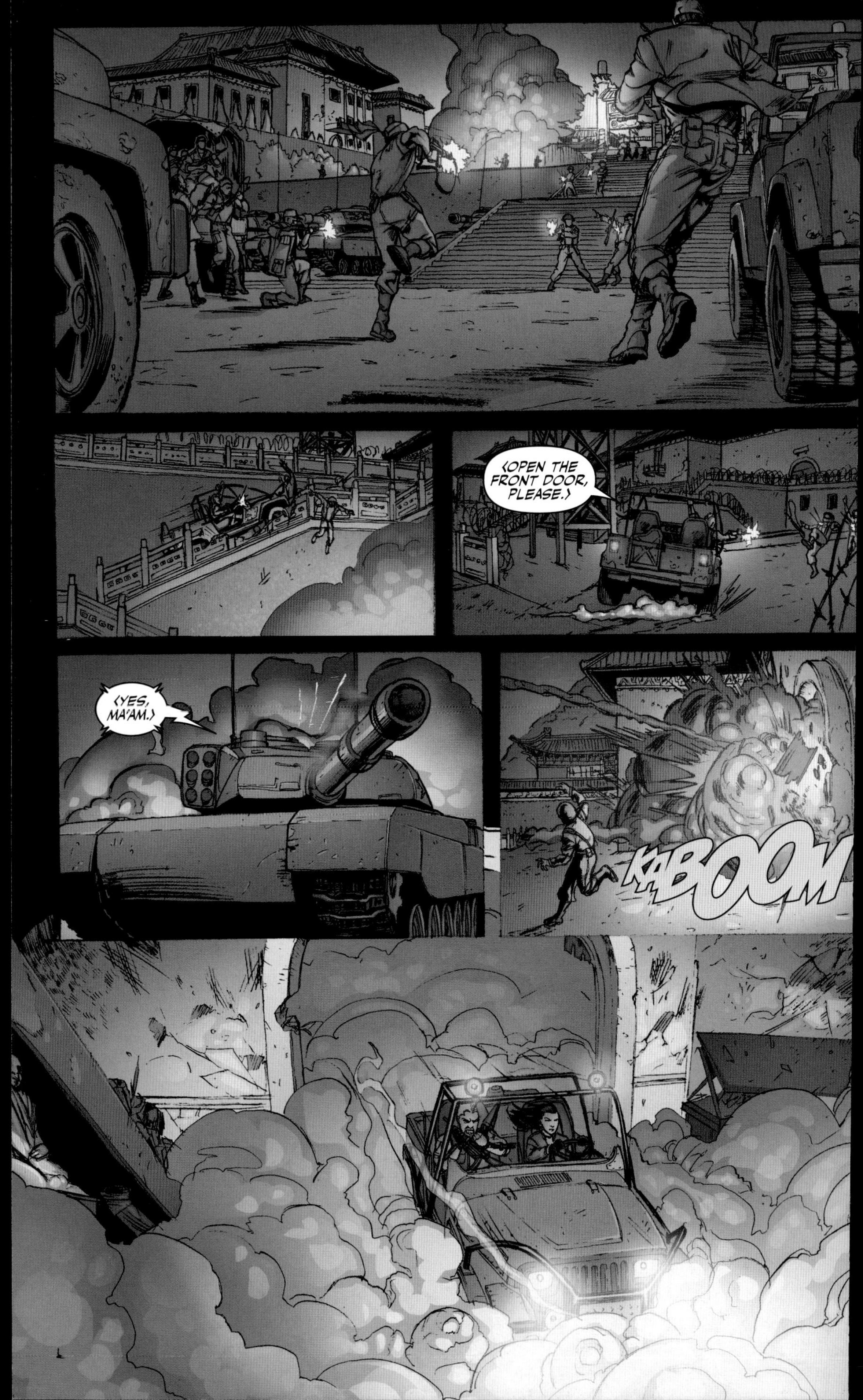
‹OPEN THE FRONT DOOR, PLEASE.›
‹YES, MA'AM.›
KABOOM

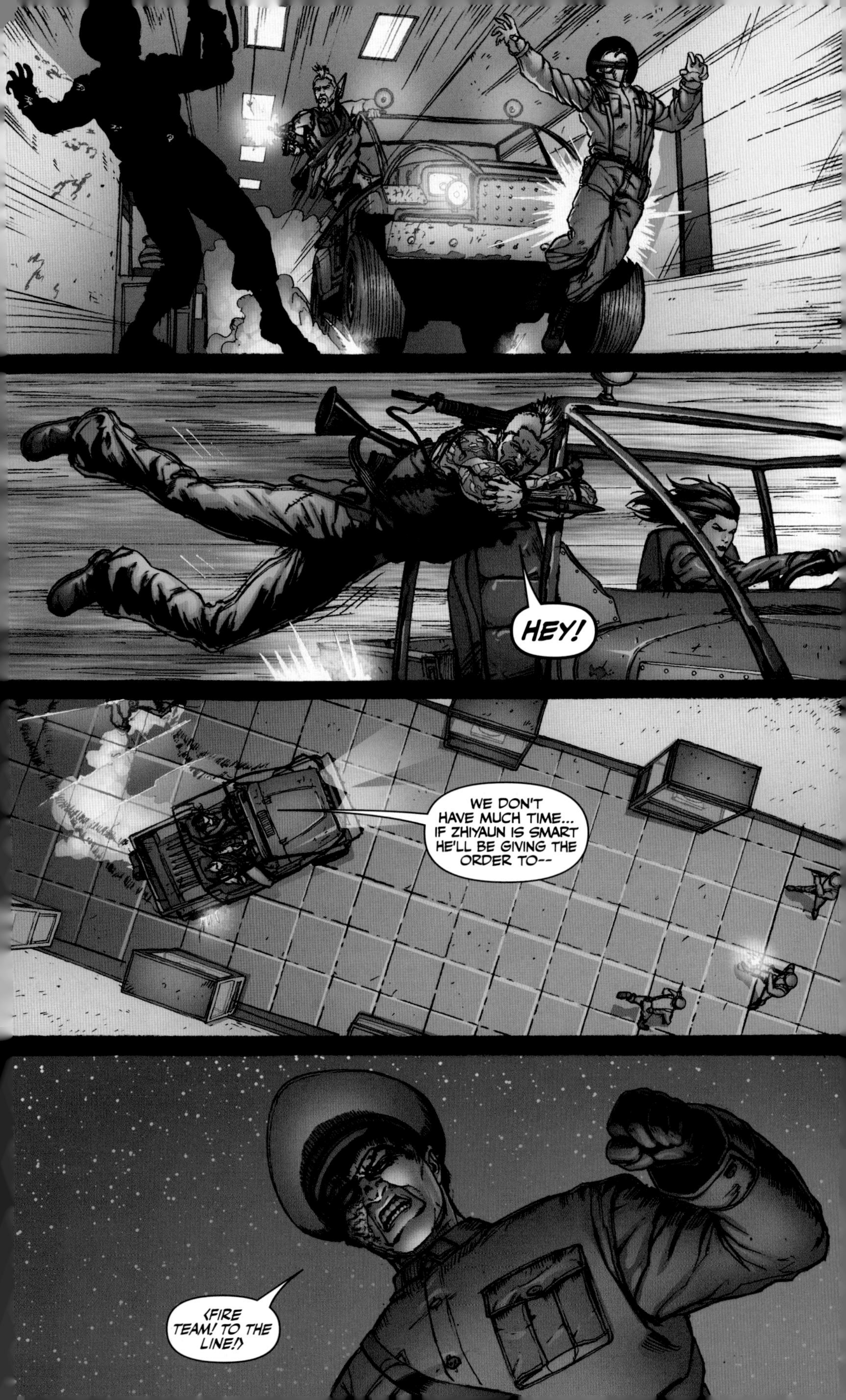
HEY!
WE DON'T HAVE MUCH TIME... IF ZHIYAUN IS SMART HE'LL BE GIVING THE ORDER TO--
‹FIRE TEAM! TO THE LINE!›

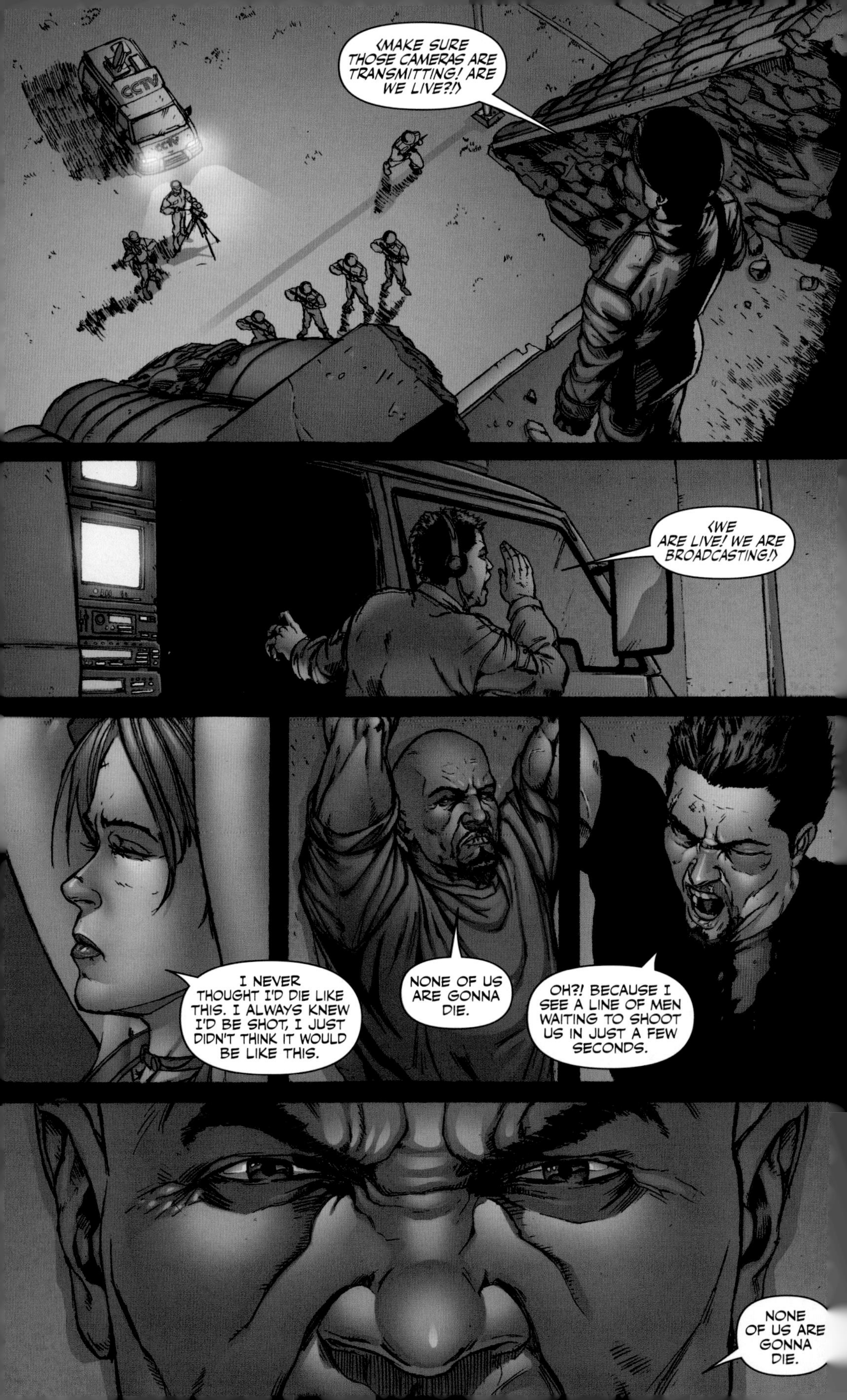
‹MAKE SURE THOSE CAMERAS ARE TRANSMITTING! ARE WE LIVE?!›
‹WE ARE LIVE! WE ARE BROADCASTING!›
I NEVER THOUGHT I'D DIE LIKE THIS. I ALWAYS KNEW I'D BE SHOT, I JUST DIDN'T THINK IT WOULD BE LIKE THIS.
NONE OF US ARE GONNA DIE.
OH?! BECAUSE I SEE A LINE OF MEN WAITING TO SHOOT US IN JUST A FEW SECONDS.
NONE OF US ARE GONNA DIE.

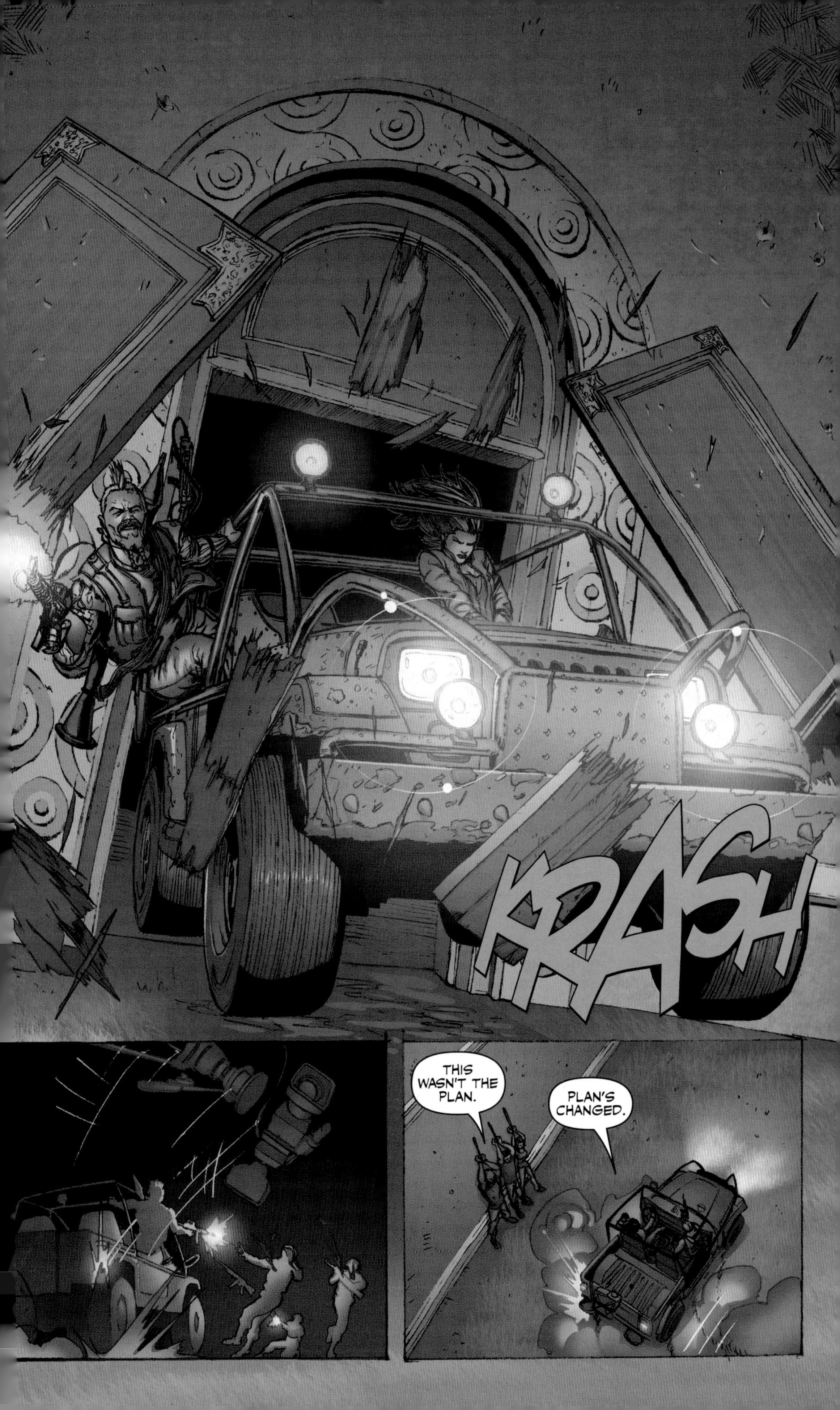
KRASH
THIS WASN'T THE PLAN.
PLAN'S CHANGED.

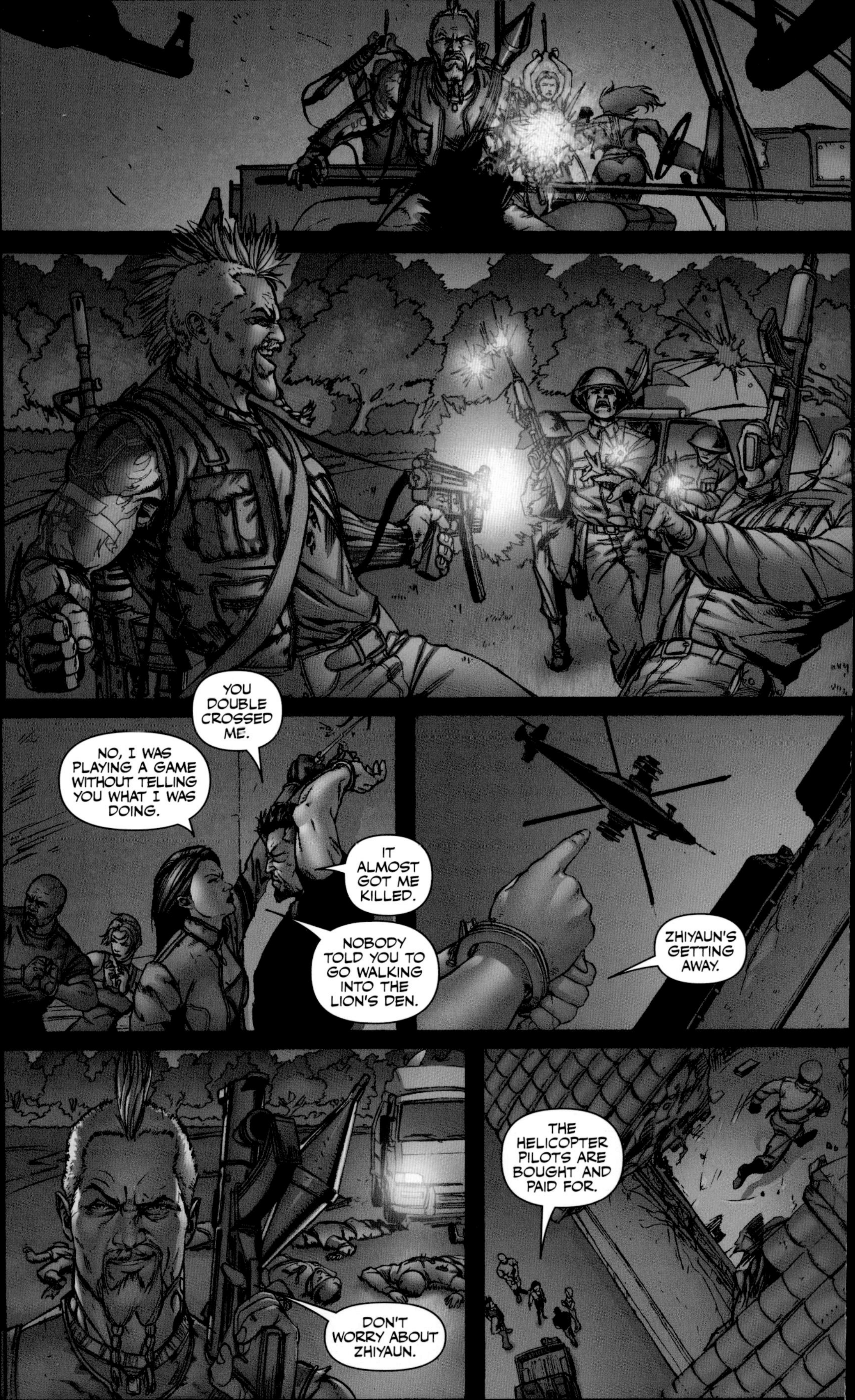
YOU DOUBLE CROSSED ME.
NO, I WAS PLAYING A GAME WITHOUT TELLING YOU WHAT I WAS DOING.
IT ALMOST GOT ME KILLED.
NOBODY TOLD YOU TO GO WALKING INTO THE LION'S DEN.
ZHIYAUN'S GETTING AWAY.
DON'T WORRY ABOUT ZHIYAUN.
THE HELICOPTER PILOTS ARE BOUGHT AND PAID FOR.

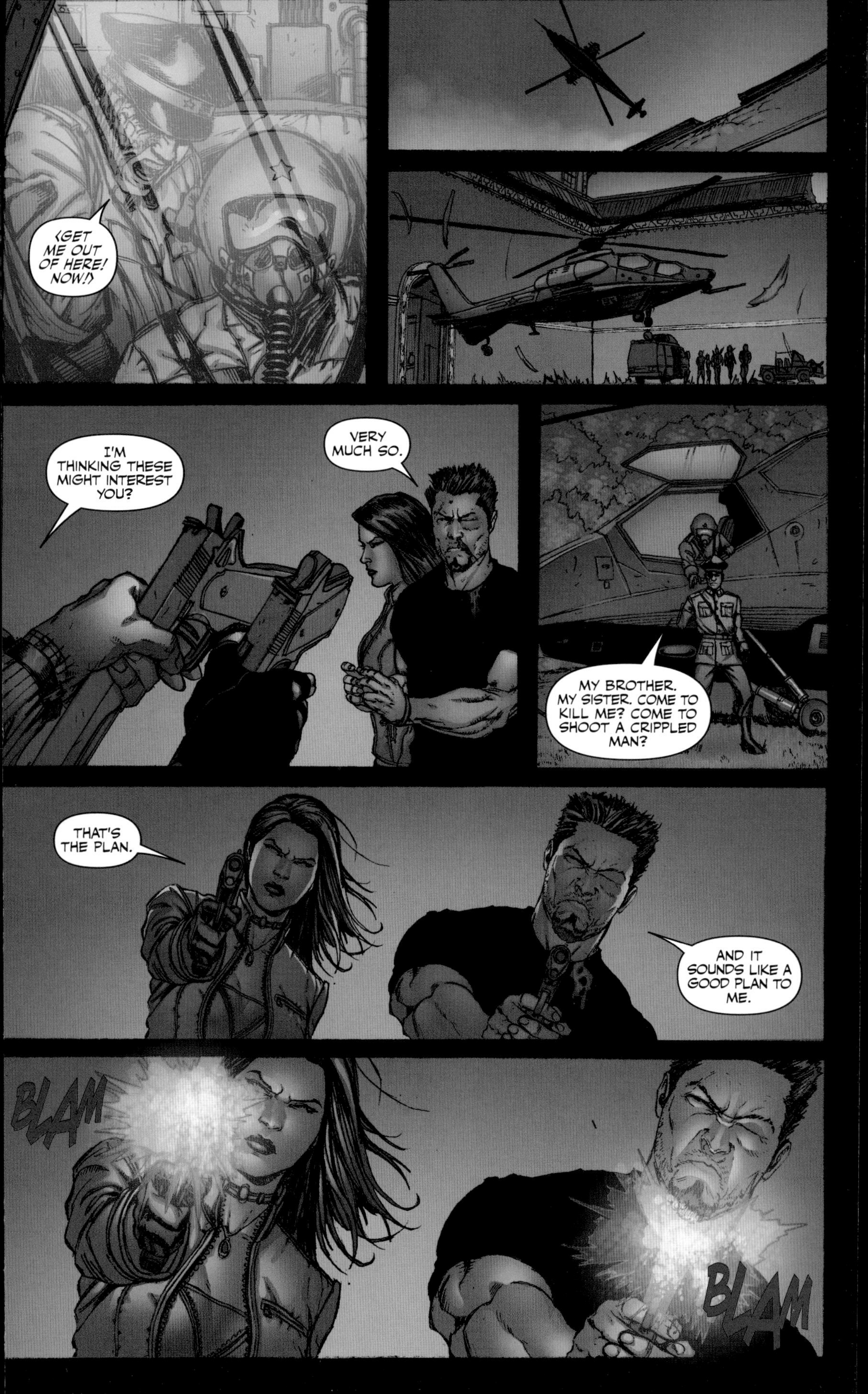
‹GET ME OUT OF HERE! NOW!›
I'M THINKING THESE MIGHT INTEREST YOU?
VERY MUCH SO.
MY BROTHER. MY SISTER. COME TO KILL ME? COME TO SHOOT A CRIPPLED MAN?
THAT'S THE PLAN.
AND IT SOUNDS LIKE A GOOD PLAN TO ME.
BLAM
BLAM

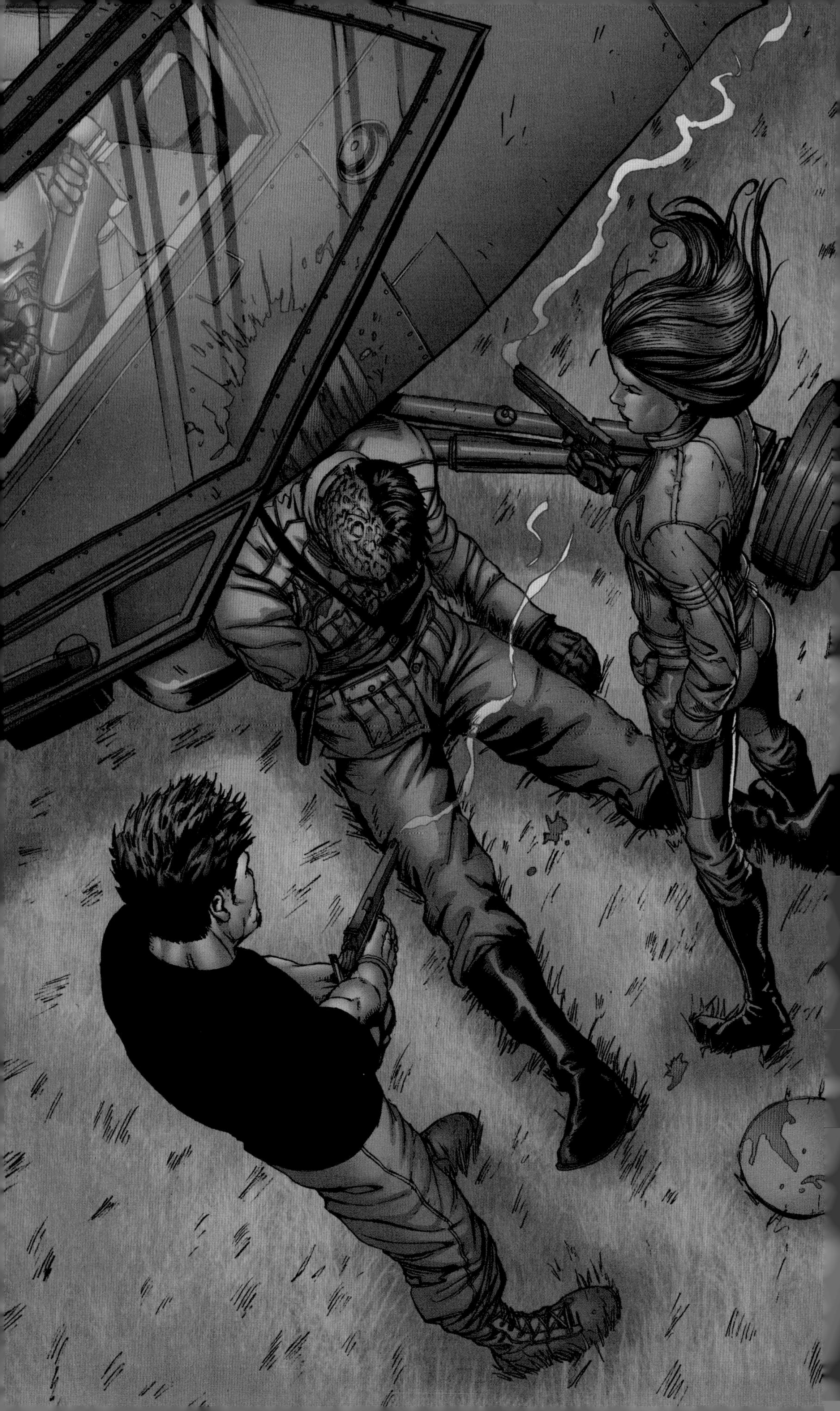

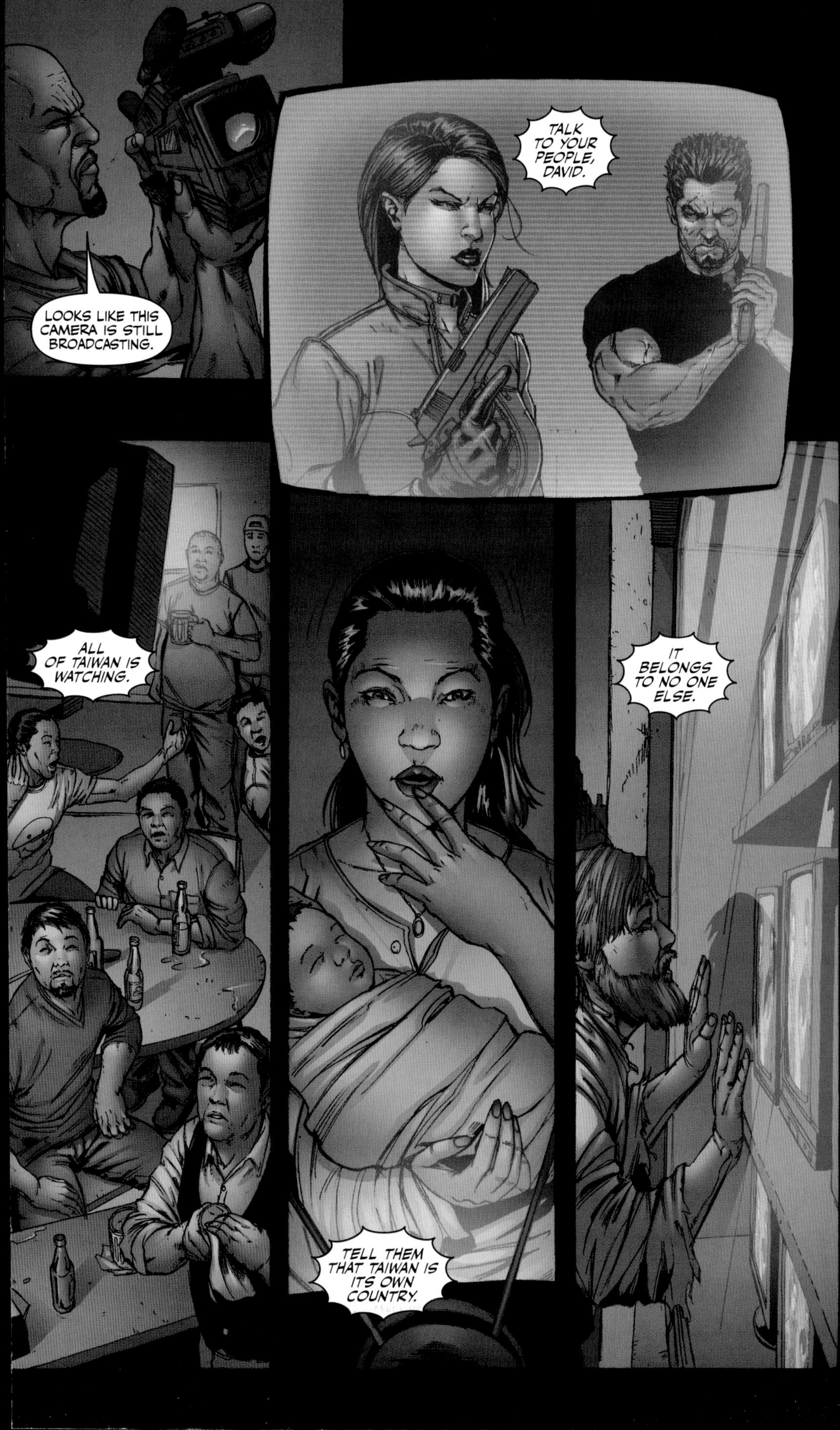
LOOKS LIKE THIS CAMERA IS STILL BROADCASTING.
TALK TO YOUR PEOPLE, DAVID.
ALL OF TAIWAN IS WATCHING.
TELL THEM THAT TAIWAN IS ITS OWN COUNTRY.
IT BELONGS TO NO ONE ELSE.

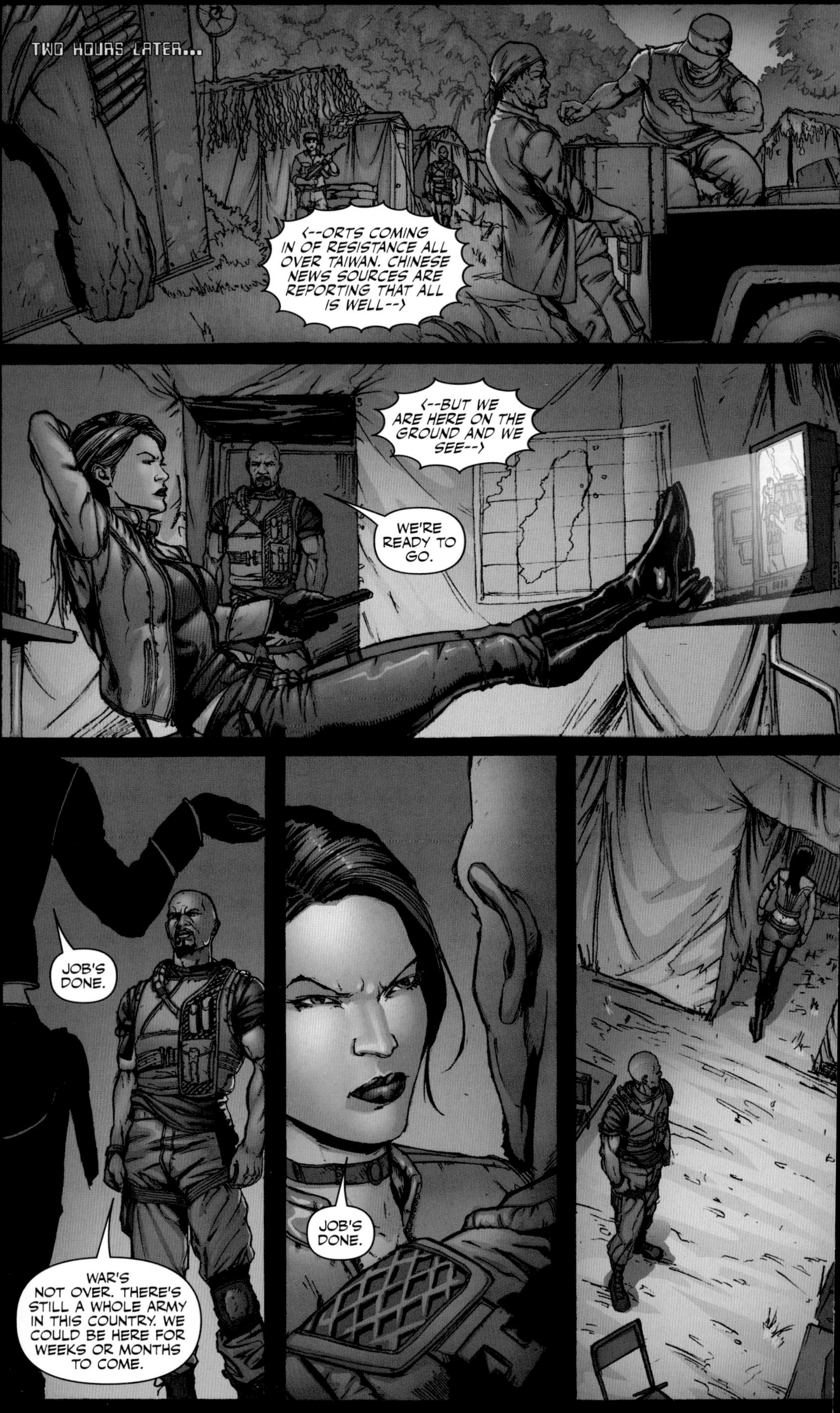
TWO HOURS LATER...
<--ORTS COMING IN OF RESISTANCE ALL OVER TAIWAN. CHINESE NEWS SOURCES ARE REPORTING THAT ALL IS WELL-->
<--BUT WE ARE HERE ON THE GROUND AND WE SEE-->
WE'RE READY TO GO.
JOB'S DONE.
WAR'S NOT OVER. THERE'S STILL A WHOLE ARMY IN THIS COUNTRY. WE COULD BE HERE FOR WEEKS OR MONTHS TO COME.
JOB'S DONE.

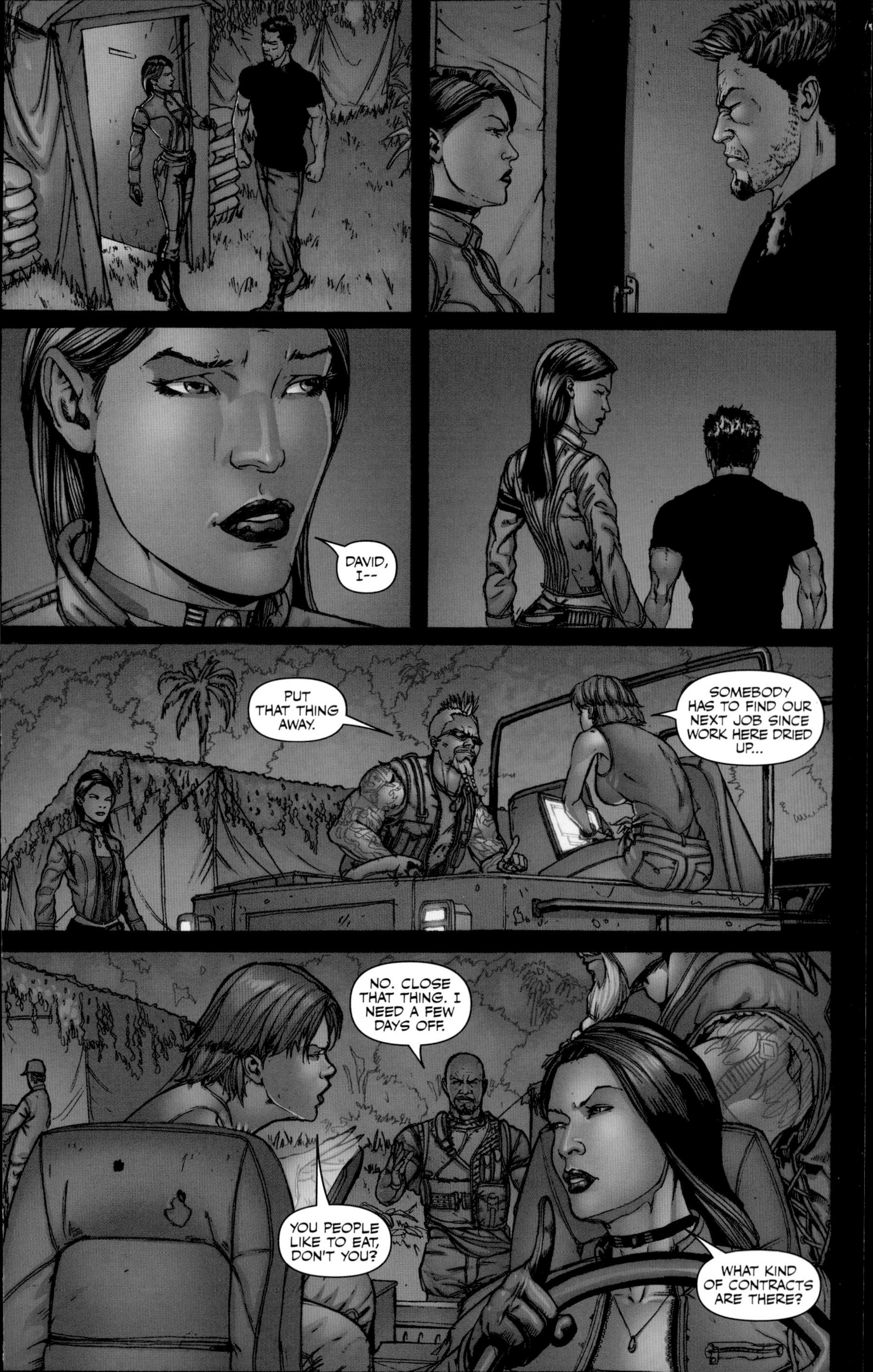
DAVID, I--
PUT THAT THING AWAY.
SOMEBODY HAS TO FIND OUR NEXT JOB SINCE WORK HERE DRIED UP...
NO. CLOSE THAT THING. I NEED A FEW DAYS OFF.
YOU PEOPLE LIKE TO EAT, DON'T YOU?
WHAT KIND OF CONTRACTS ARE THERE?

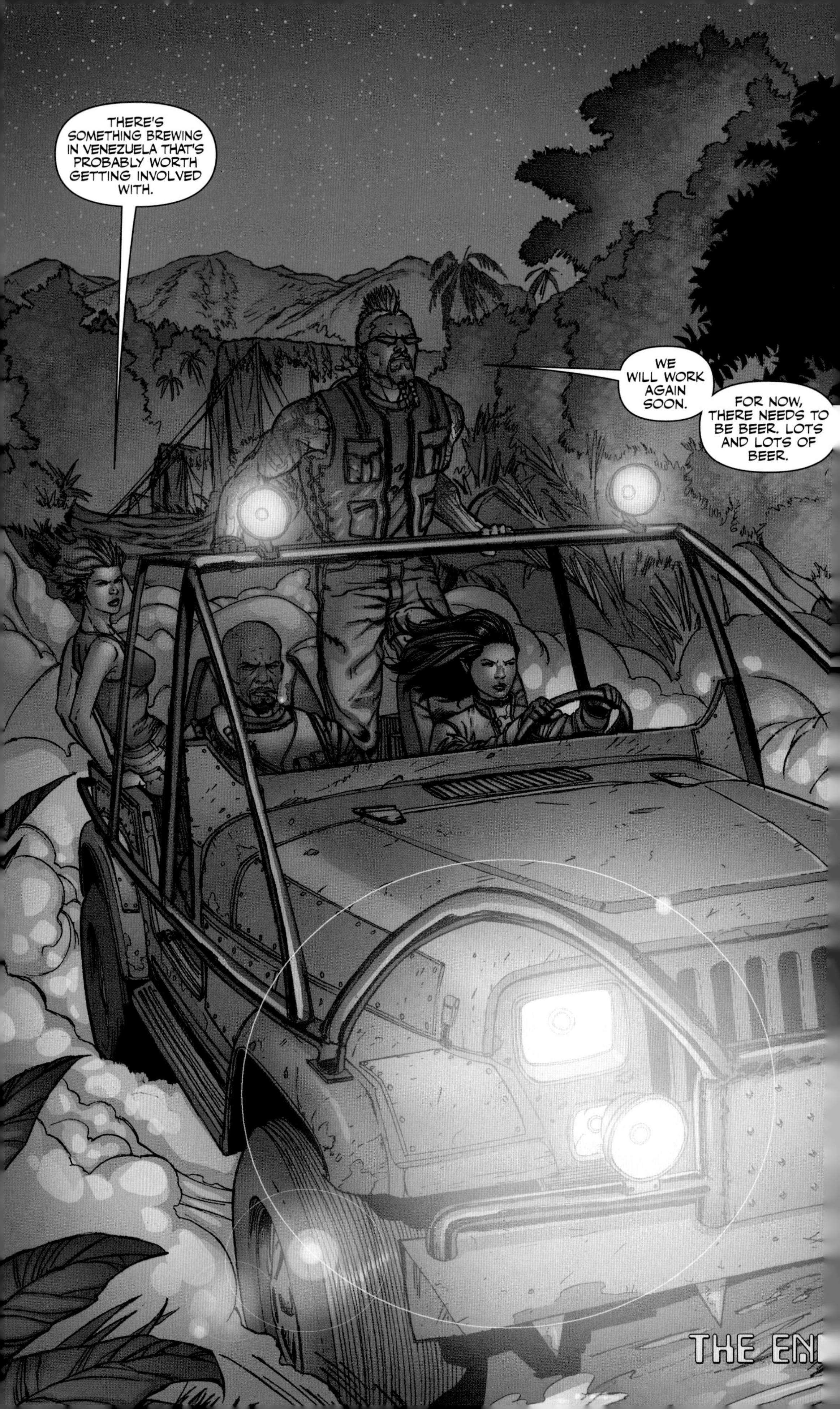

THERE'S SOMETHING BREWING IN VENEZUELA THAT'S PROBABLY WORTH GETTING INVOLVED WITH.
WE WILL WORK AGAIN SOON.
FOR NOW, THERE NEEDS TO BE BEER. LOTS AND LOTS OF BEER.
THE EN

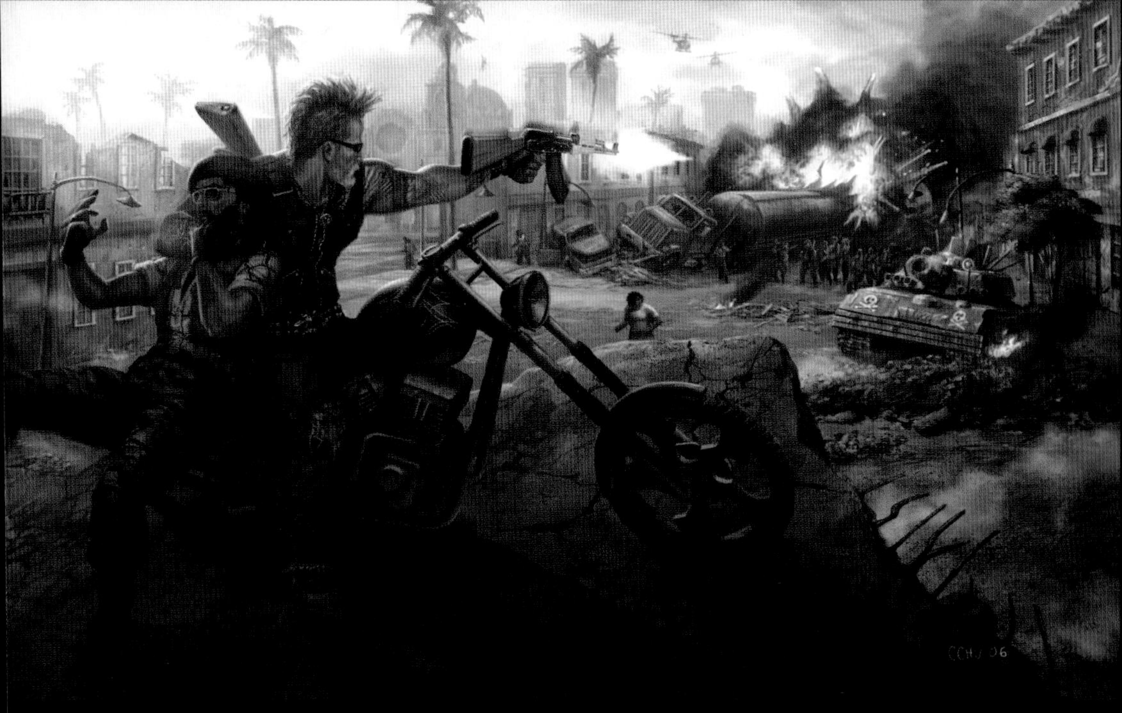

artist: ***court chu***

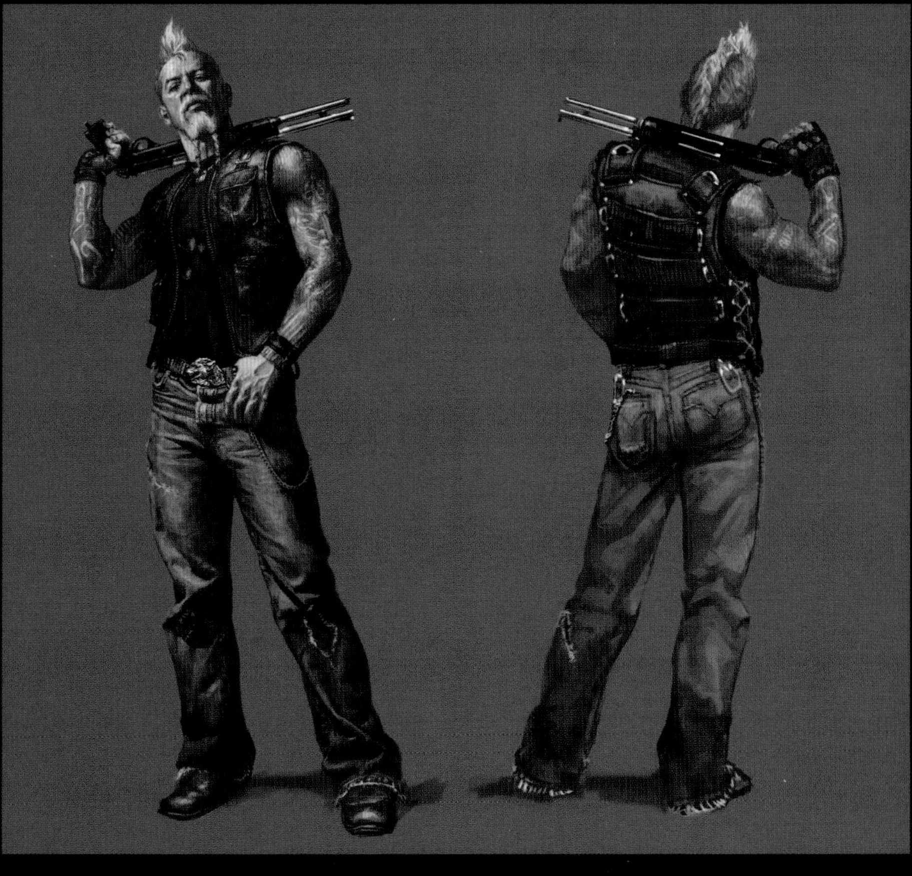

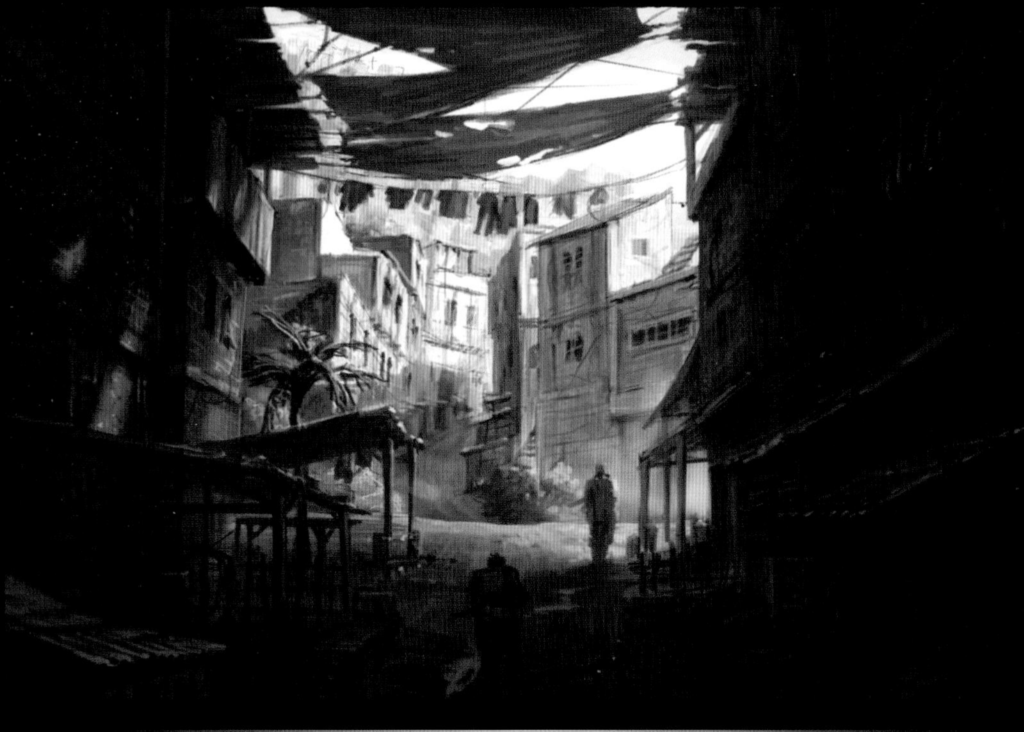

name: **shanty painting 02** artist: **court chu**

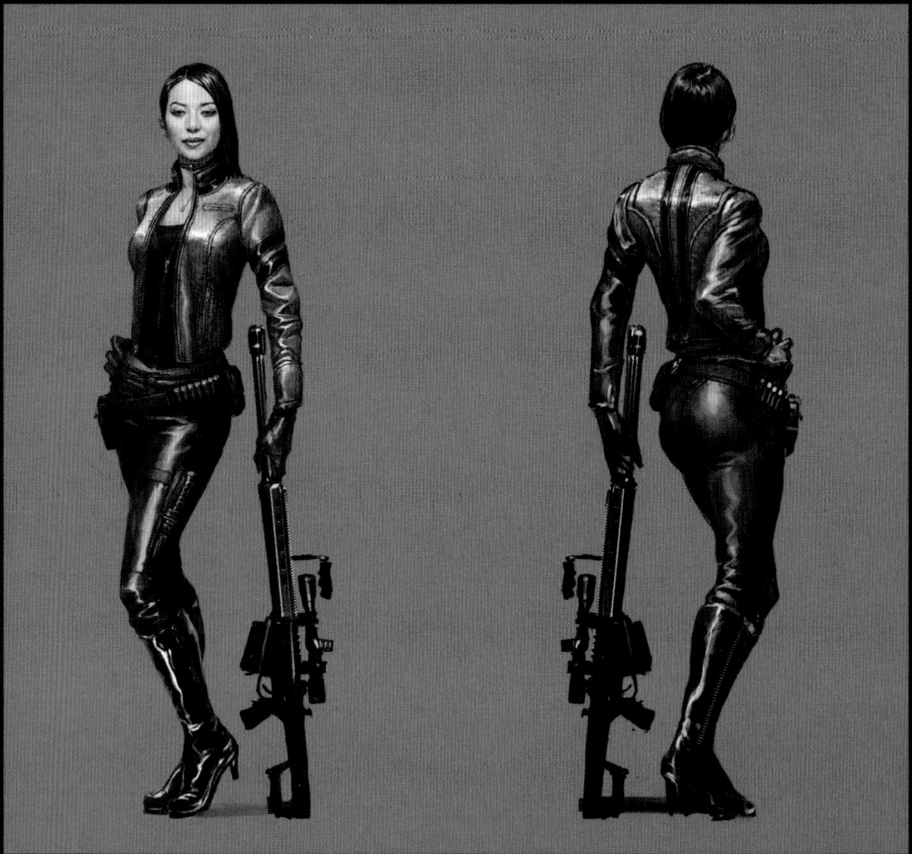

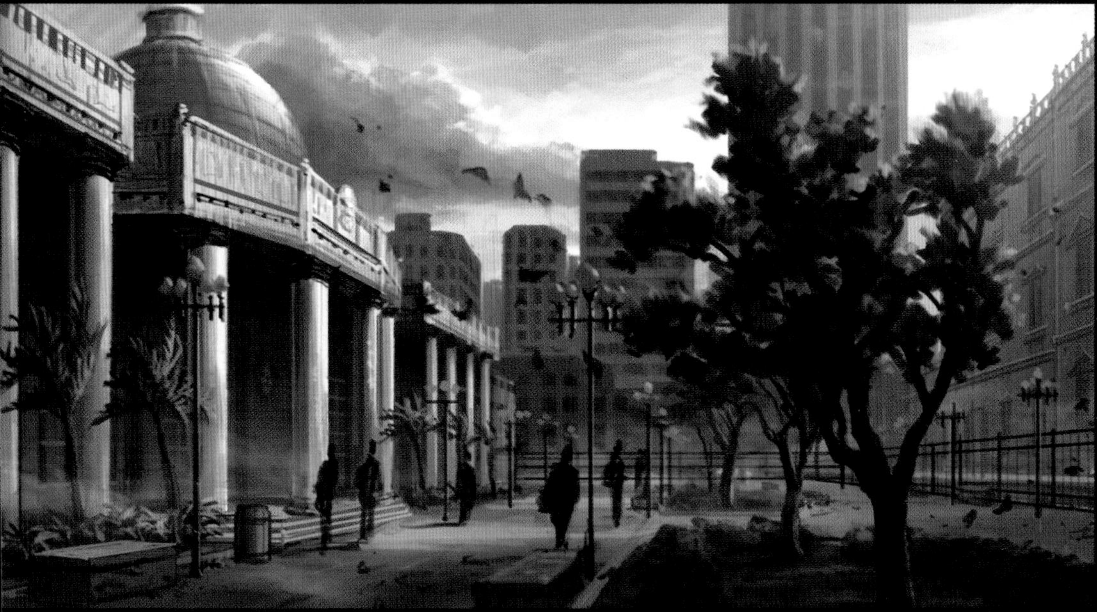

artist: **court chu**

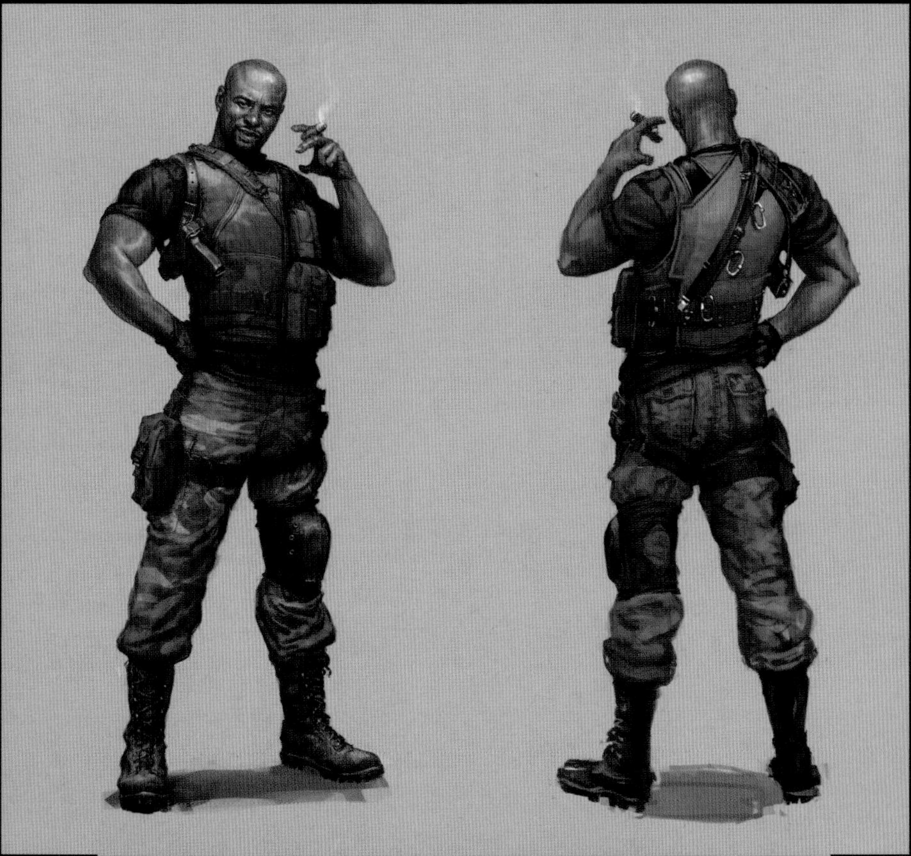

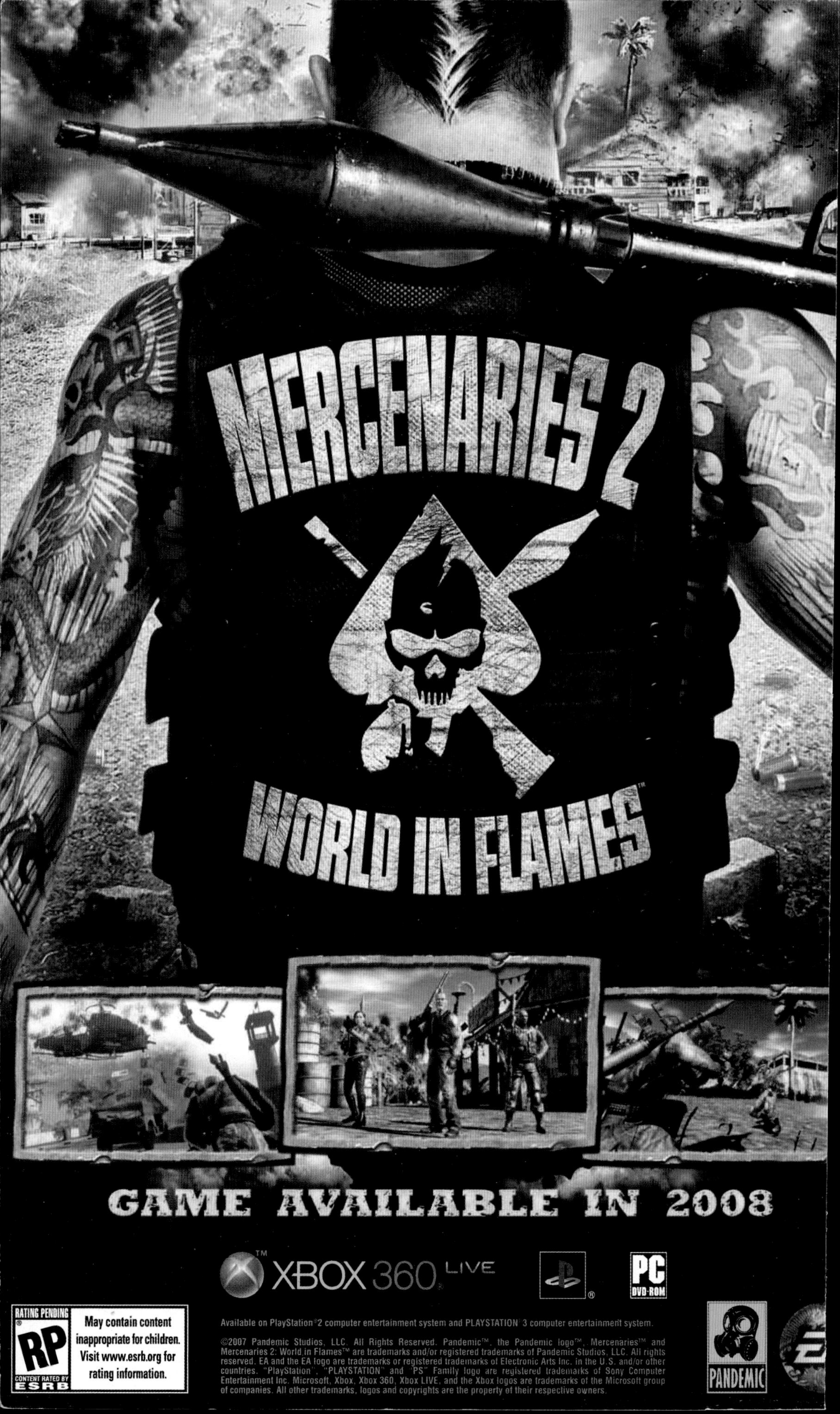
MERCENARIES 2
WORLD IN FLAMES™
GAME AVAILABLE IN 2008
XBOX 360 LIVE
PC DVD-ROM
RATING PENDING
RP
CONTENT RATED BY ESRB
May contain content inappropriate for children. Visit www.esrb.org for rating information.
Available on PlayStation®2 computer entertainment system and PLAYSTATION®3 computer entertainment system.
©2007 Pandemic Studios, LLC. All Rights Reserved. Pandemic™, the Pandemic logo™, Mercenaries™ and Mercenaries 2: World in Flames™ are trademarks and/or registered trademarks of Pandemic Studios, LLC. All rights reserved. EA and the EA logo are trademarks or registered trademarks of Electronic Arts Inc. in the U.S. and/or other countries. "PlayStation", "PLAYSTATION" and "PS" Family logo are registered trademarks of Sony Computer Entertainment Inc. Microsoft, Xbox, Xbox 360, Xbox LIVE, and the Xbox logos are trademarks of the Microsoft group of companies. All other trademarks, logos and copyrights are the property of their respective owners.
PANDEMIC